PEOPLE CALLED
LADAKH

Through the Lens of Culture and Everyday Lives

Curated by
Nisha Nair and Shashi Velath

Published by Westland Non-Fiction, an imprint of Westland Books, a division of Nasadiya Technologies Private Limited, in 2024

No. 269/2B, First Floor, 'Irai Arul', Vimalraj Street, Nethaji Nagar, Alapakkam Main Road, Maduravoyal, Chennai 600095

Westland, the Westland logo, Westland Non-Fiction and the Westland Non-Fiction logo are the trademarks of Nasadiya Technologies Private Limited, or its affiliates.

Copyright © Nisha Nair, 2024

ISBN: 9789360456566

10 9 8 7 6 5 4 3 2 1

The views and opinions expressed in this work are the authors' own and the facts are as reported by them, and the publisher is in no way liable for the same.

Typeset by Riddhima Khedkar
Editorial Assistant: Saylee Soundalgekar
Printed at Thomson Press (India) Ltd

*Dedicated to the individuals and communities
striving to sustain the unique Ladakhi culture*

Credits: Jiten Desai

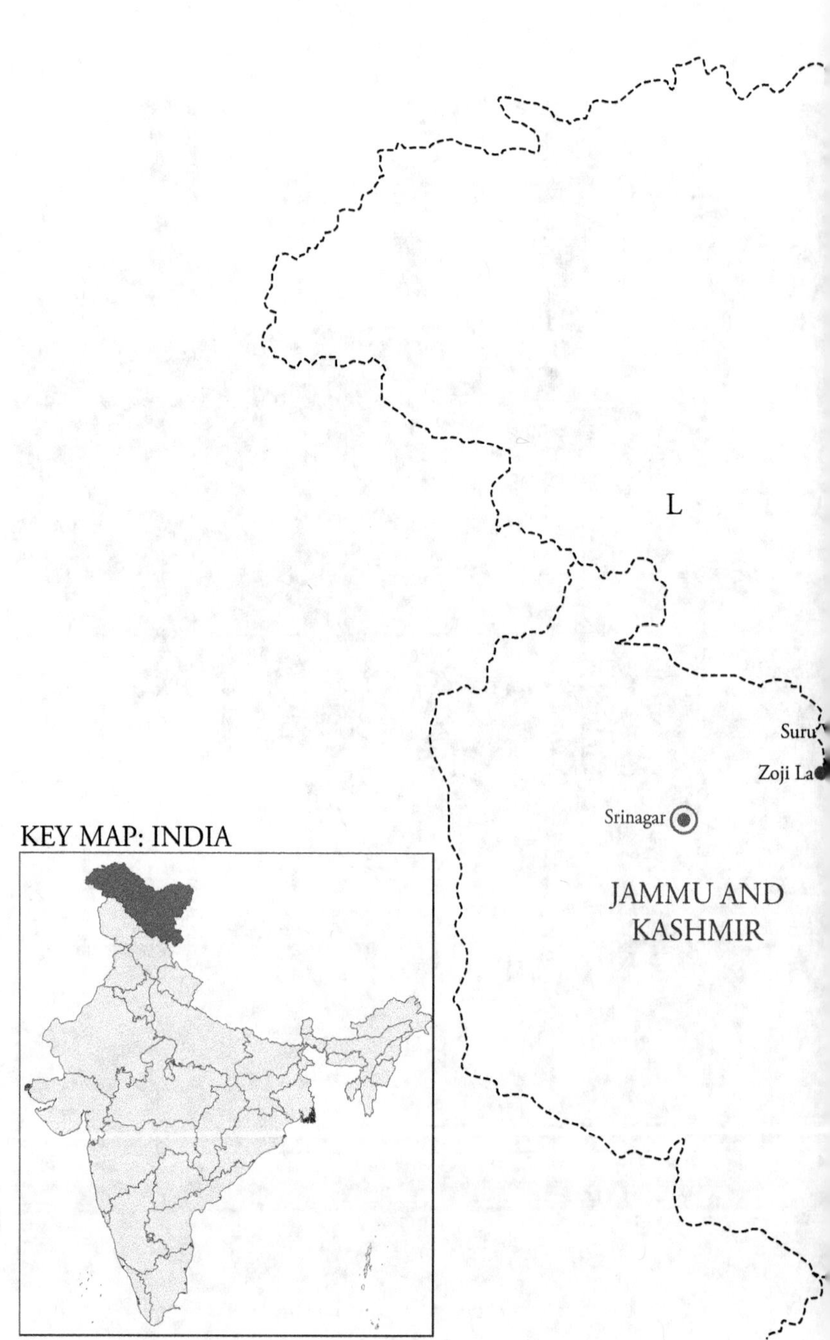

L
Suru
Zoji La
Srinagar
JAMMU AND KASHMIR
KEY MAP: INDIA

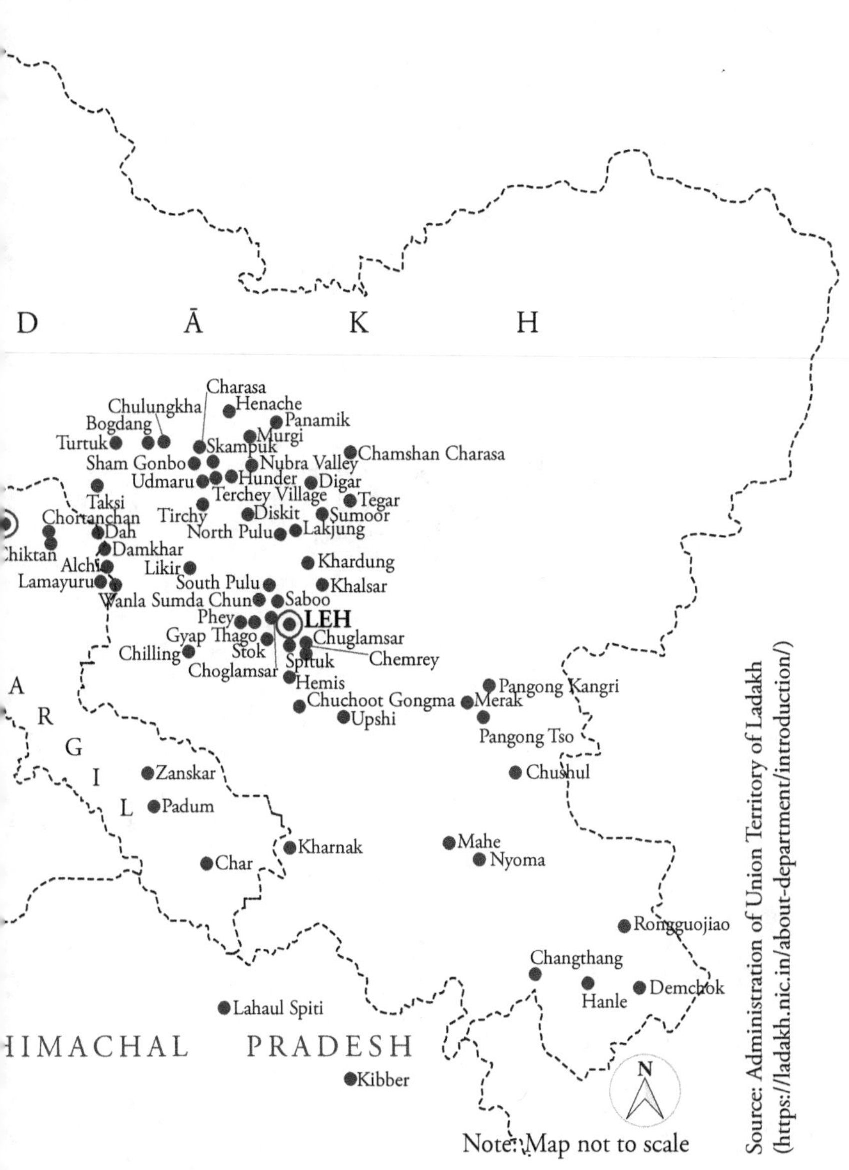

LADĀKH, UT
Administrative Boundary
D   Ā   K   H
Charasa
Chulungkha   Henache
Bogdang   Panamik
Turtuk   Murgi
Skampuk
Sham Gonbo   Nubra Valley   Chamshan Charasa
Udmaru   Hunder   Digar
Terchey Village   Tegar
Taksi   Tirchy   Diskit   Sumoor
Chortanchan   North Pulu   Lakjung
Dah
Chiktan   Damkhar
Alchi   Likir   Khardung
Lamayuru   South Pulu   Khalsar
Wanla Sumda Chun   Saboo
Phey   LEH
Gyap Thago   Chuglamsar
Chilling   Stok   Chemrey
Choglamsar   Spituk
Hemis   Pangong Kangri
Chuchoot Gongma   Merak
Upshi
Pangong Tso
A
R
G
I   Zanskar   Chushul
L   Padum
Kharnak   Mahe
Char   Nyoma
Rongguojiao
Changthang
Hanle   Demchok
Lahaul Spiti
HIMACHAL   PRADESH
Kibber
N
Note: Map not to scale

Contents

Introduction

Nisha Nair and Shashi Velath

Ladakh, nestled within the majestic embrace of the Himalayas, is a region that captivates the imagination with its rugged beauty. However, the story of Ladakh is more than breathtaking landscapes, crystal-clear skies, high mountain passes, thrilling adventure activities, Buddhist monasteries and festivals. It is the story of the various people, communities, practices and traditions that have made it what it is. It is also intertwined with their spiritual and reverential relationship with nature. It is the story of a resilient culture that has persisted as well as transformed through the ups and downs of history.

As a Union Territory of India, with a modest population of 274,289 as per the 2011 census, Ladakh, celebrated as the 'Land of High Passes', offers a unique blend of scenic beauty and cultural vibrancy. The transition to Union Territory status in 2019, following the abrogation of Articles 370 and 35A, marked a significant milestone in Ladakh's history, ushering in a new era of socio-political and cultural integration with India. The cultural landscape of Ladakh is a harmonious blend of Tibetan Buddhism and Indo–Aryan influences, reflected in its monasteries, festivals and everyday life. The region's spiritual aura, with Buddhism at its core, shapes its social and cultural ethos. Monasteries like Hemis, Thiksey and Lamayuru are not just places of worship but custodians of rich historical art, literature and traditional knowledge. Festivals such as Losar (Ladakhi new year) and Hemis Tsechu showcase Ladakh's vibrant cultural heritage, drawing tourists and scholars alike. Ladakh's architectural landscape, with its fortresses, traditional houses and Buddhist stupas, reflects a blend of Tibetan and Indian influences, optimised for harsh climatic conditions. The region's cuisine, revealing Tibetan influence and adaptation to high-altitude living, is intertwined with Ladakh's cultural rituals and festivals. Also, as Ladakh strides towards a sustainable future, initiatives like 'Carbon Neutral Ladakh' and the establishment of India's first dark sky reserve at Hanley highlight the region's commitment to sustainable development and environmental conservation. These efforts are crucial aspects of Ladakh's cultural narrative, demonstrating how the region is weaving the thread of cultural and environmental consciousness into its developmental narrative without compromising its cultural and ecological integrity. This book, *People Called Ladakh*, is a conscious attempt to look at 'culture'—both past and present, tangible and intangible, inherited and evolving—through people's everyday experiences, as a lens to understand Ladakh.

People Called Ladakh is a window into the heart and soul of this enigmatic land. In this anthology of thirty-two stories, we embark on a journey through the alleys of Ladakhi life, exploring its diverse facets, from intricate social dynamics to age-old arts and crafts, and rhythms of everyday life in Ladakh. It is an anthology of these stories of culture and the everyday through people's experiences, spanning the region's geography, from Leh to Kargil. The book is also unique because the sixteen authors who have contributed to the anthology come from diverse backgrounds—researchers, cultural practitioners, local architects, anthropology students, as well as a Buddhist nun. Through the lens of 'people' and 'empathy', the thirty-two stories of *People Called Ladakh* paint a contemporary picture of the everyday culture in the region. Thus, this book aims to encapsulate the voices of Ladakhis, ensuring that the region's narrative is authentically shaped by those intimately connected to its land and culture.

In essence, this book is more than merely a cultural document; it is a strategic intervention that celebrates, preserves and promotes the unique cultural landscape of Ladakh within the Union of India. This testament to the region's enduring spirit and its contributions to the Indian cultural mosaic is an essential read for those interested in cultural preservation, sustainability and the rich tapestry of human diversity. It ensures that the lessons, beauty and challenges of Ladakh's journey continue to inspire and educate future generations, solidifying Ladakh's role and significance in the broader context of India and the world.

Credits: Author

A 'tSelbu' Full of Happiness

Own Ali Kaizen

Manjushri, the embodiment of wisdom, hark!
The gods, the Lhu and owner spirits of Mother Earth hark!
May a hundred plants grow from one seed!
May a thousand grow from two!
May all the grains be twins!
—A Ladakhi sowing song

Far from the hustle and bustle of the world, Ajang Husain sits comfortably on his jute mattress made out of the rice sacs that he's collected over the years. Next to him sits a Tibetan cylindrical flask, a cup filled to the brim with butter tea and a Philips radio set that seems like his companion for life. His son had got him this valuable radio set when he was in the Ladakh Scouts. Now, as he is retired from the force, Ajang is relieved, for these days he gets a helping hand in the fields and at home. The butter tea keeps him hydrated for the day, and the radio is his source of entertainment on the days when he is all by himself with no one to share his conversations with. His village, located at a distant place from the town, is a small place with only around ten families in total. The land is quite fertile and cultivable. It is considered

'Raltan', as plantations like apricots, walnuts, apples, and peaches grow here (Raltan in Ladakhi signifies an area or land deemed fertile and conducive for the growth and production of different kinds of vegetation). But, despite it being heaven compared to the relatively barren villages in Ladakh, the people of this village, mostly the youth, have migrated to the town of Kargil for their education and livelihood. This is a major point of concern as there are no standard schools in his village owing to its remoteness and inaccessibility.

The village has yet to get any kind of network connectivity. Almost all the nearby villages have had the infrastructure for quite a while. A couple of homes have managed to get a landline installed, which serves as a lifeline for the whole village. But, despite all these difficulties, Ajang and his like-minded villagers live here with great contentment and satisfaction, without any major complaints. The only complaint they have is about their young children leaving for the nearest towns.

When asked why their children prefer to go to the towns rather than stay in the villages, Ajang says, with disappointment, 'There are many reasons for it, but according to me, they go because they want to earn a livelihood with less struggle. If they do what it takes in their own fields, they can get a decent livelihood from here as well, but alas! They're fascinated more by the fast-moving world.'

Farming in Ladakh is difficult, thanks to the harsh climate, the short agricultural season and the wild, barren landscape. Yet, the region has created wonders and stands as an example of sustainable living. 'We have created small dams and channels in the field,' says Ajang. 'The land is always all set to receive water from the melting snow. We had terraced our fields with stone walls. You should visit in the summer. The shades of green and the blue of the Indus, against the barren landscape, are remarkable.'

I ask, 'What is that purple colour in the fields?' He replies with a chuckle, 'That's just a highlight in the canvas!' Later, he explains that the colourful highlights of purple, mauve and yellow are grasses, clover, herbs and fodder for the cattle. I go for a long walk in the field with him. While he expresses his concerns, he's heavily engrossed in readying the curved base to start making his 'tSepo', also known as 'tSelbu', the local cart or basket that people carry on their backs for varied purposes. The women mostly use it to carry their toddlers while they're asleep and to carry things like gravel, grass or timber while working outdoors. It is so multipurpose that every household has at least a couple of tSepos in their homes. Savouring his tea while braiding the strands of his tSepo, he reminisces about how they used to love their land and cultivate it with great dedication. He says, 'The whole of the summer used to be so busy and rewarding. We used to sow wheat at the beginning of the season, then after harvesting it, buckwheat, and by the end of August apricots and apples were collected.'

We continue walking around the fields. Yet another proven heritage that has stood the test of time and is still used today is the rantak—a traditional water mill of Ladakh. 'In the summer,' Ajang says, 'you see snow melting and hundreds of streams taking shape. Running ferociously, they form rivers for the country. What we did is, we tapped this water. We built rantak.' The water-driven mill is used to convert the kinetic energy of the moving water into mechanical energy. The fast-moving water forces the turbine to rotate, which further leads to the rotational motion of the grinding stone upon the stationary one. 'Nowadays, even though processes like ploughing and threshing have been widely mechanised, the young generation doesn't want to get their hands dirty. They now prefer going to the cities with their families.'

As the clock approaches 7 p.m., Ajang leaves the strands of rchispiang (a type of shrub to make tSepo) down and rests his back on the boulders, taking the radio set on his shoulder, close to his ear, listening keenly to the noise while tuning into different signal ranges. After moving the tuner for a few seconds, he raises his eyebrows; he can hear a woman speaking Ladakhi. After making it sound clearer, he tells me, 'This is 340.8 MHz, where we get the news.' He says that he never misses this bulletin apart from a few other programmes like *Fauji Farmaish*.

During the day, most of his time is spent in making the 'tSepo' as it is a long and tiring process in itself. Even before he starts the process of making it, he has to first get the rchispiang ready. The rchispiang is braided to make the tSepo. The shrub has to be kept in a water body, like a lake or stream, for about twenty days before use, so as to keep its agility intact. When it is agile enough, it is further softened and braided along the hard curved base to give it the final shape. When completed, the tSepo takes somewhat like a conical shape with four corners. To make it comfortable to be carried on the backs, a strap is further attached to it. Ajang says that he learned this skill in his adulthood from his late father.

'Back in the day,' he says, 'every other person used to have these skills of weaving a tSepo or making a pabu. It is this generation that is reluctant to learn these things. Back then it was considered very basic, and every person was supposed to know about it all. Like the art of making a tSepo, every other art is gradually disappearing in Ladakh.' Offering me a cup of butter tea, he says, 'As having these skills was very common in those times, they wouldn't earn any income, but they were more independent in their lives. Most of his livelihood came from selling apricots and apples in the summer season, rather than making tSepos. 'In addition to tSepos we also have shak, zungba, rzgeem, saddle, khem, khaczhay, gourgur, butter churner, plough, smeing, rbhat and grookook.'

The winters, like any other place in Ladakh, would be cold and harsh in his village too, keeping them confined to their homes for the whole winter. Thus, he would collect the cow-dung cakes and the timber wood in the tSepo he had made in summer, and he would light the hearth, making his little mud house cosy and warm. 'Let winter come. For nothing is wasted,' he says, naively commenting on the trending subject of circular economy and the Ladakhi approach to resource utilisation in the changing climate. 'Animal dung becomes fuel, human dung goes to the fields (the traditional Ladakhi toilet is an efficient composting design), and even old gonchas (a type of clothing) may be used to patch irrigation channels. The scattered and meagre wild plants are also used for fuel, fibre and labour. 'Which lifestyle is more sustainable, then?' Ajang asks.

Are All the People of Changthang Nomads?

Spalzen Angmo and Sunetro Ghosal

Angmo (A): Why did you visit Changthang recently?

Sunetro (S): Well, I had visited Hanley to observe the establishment of the Hanley Dark Sky Reserve that is expected to benefit local communities and the environment through the preservation of the night sky. The night sky in Hanley is one of the darkest in the world.

A: But I can see stars in the sky in Leh, too.

S: Yes, but those are only the brightest stars and planets. Most of Ladakh is suffering from light pollution like other parts of the world.

A: So why is Hanley different?

S: Possibly because local communities are still practising sustainable lifestyles.

A: Oh! Are all the people in Changthang nomads?

S: What did you observe when you visited Changthang?

A: I noticed some houses with sheepdogs along with goats and sheep. I did not see any rebos (tents), but everyone says that people in Changthang are nomads.

S: Changthang is a high-altitude area located above the agriculture zone for this latitude. This means farming is very difficult in this area.

A: But I did see farmlands…

S: Yes, but the yield is very low.

A: How do people live then?

S: Some agriculture is done in Changthang but a majority of the people herd livestock.

A: So, they live in rebos?

S: They have a home in their village but they live in rebos along with their livestock as they move from one pasture/rangeland to the next.

A: How do they know which pasture to use?

S: The nomads in Changthang are called Changpas. They are divided into different groups with exclusive rights to specific rangelands.

A: How do they decide when to move from an area?

S: The Changpas are constantly monitoring the rangeland. When they notice that the grass in the rangeland is low, they move to prevent overgrazing. These rangelands are a very important resource for the Changpas who must conserve them.

A: How do they travel to the next pasture?

S: In the past, they would use yaks and horses to carry their rebos and luggage while they walked with the goat and sheep. Kids and lambs would be saddled on horses and yaks if they were too young for such journeys. Now, many have started using motor vehicles.

A: How do they establish camp at the new location?

S: Each pasture has a camping ground, which includes the base for tents and corral pens. Once they arrive in the new area, they repair these structures and establish camp.

A: How do they get water?

S: These camping grounds are generally near water sources such as streams. In the winter, these streams freeze and they have to break and melt the ice.

A: Wow! What sort of fuel sources do they use? There are very few trees in the area.

S: Some shrubs do grow in Changthang but the main fuel source is animal dung, i.e., droppings from goat, sheep, yak and horses.

A: That sounds like a tough life.

S: It is. Nowadays, they also use LPG cylinders.

A: And what do they eat if they are not able to grow much?

S: They generally have a meat-based diet with a lot of dairy products made from milk from their herds. In the past, they would visit Khar-gu, Serthi and Upshi to barter wool, meat and animal-based products for barley, wheat, apricots, etc.

A: And where do they buy other supplies?

S: Well, most supplies are now available in the larger villages and army canteens as well as through relatives in Leh.

A: But how do the Changpas get money to buy things?

S: They sell different products from their herd, especially raw pashm, which is in great demand.

A: What is pashm?

S: Pashm is the fine undercoat of the Changthang goats, which is used to make the famous Pashmina shawls and other products.

A: I see. If they have this important source of income, why have so many Changpas moved to Leh permanently?

S: In the past, many Changpa families did sell their herds to move to Leh. However, they later realised that they had limited opportunities in Leh.

A: Is this migration still happening?

S: The numbers are much lower now

A: But Changthang is such a beautiful area…

S: It is also very harsh. They face many challenges, including extreme cold, lack of access to medical facilities, limited job opportunities, unpredictable climatic patterns, conflicts with wildlife, etc.

A: Oh, okay. I've also seen people react negatively if you call them a Changpa. Why is that?

S: There have been a lot of negative stereotypes attached to the Changpa community by people from other parts of Ladakh, especially of them being dirty, illiterate, etc.

A: Is any of that true?

S: Not in my experience. Despite the challenging terrain, the Changpas always make an effort to maintain personal hygiene. Also, the Changpas have inherited a time-tested knowledge system to manage local rangelands. They also employ various innovative strategies to overcome the challenges they face. I feel we must respect this knowledge, cultural system and the community.

A: I remember, in school, people would regard Changpa students as being different. I have also heard people claim that Changpas are not very polite as they do not meet many people and spend more time with their animals…why are there so many negative stereotypes?

S. What was your experience in Changthang?

A. I remember one Abi-ley who seemed a little overwhelmed when we asked to camp near her house. This made me think that the stereotypes are true. But then, we met an Ane-ley who was very warm, welcoming and helpful.

S: Ladakh is a diverse society and each community has its own unique culture and dialect, though elements of it are shared with other communities.

A: Yes, I remember when we used to have social gatherings in the evening, many local youth would also join us. They seemed fascinated by how different and yet similar we were.

S: That is interesting. How many of your classmates from the Changpa community have since returned home?

A: They would go home for vacations, but most of them are still studying. Why do you ask?

S: Education has been a mixed experience for the Changpas. They are acutely aware of the importance of education. Some send their children to nomadic residential schools in Changthang while others send them to schools in Leh and even outside Ladakh.

A: Yes, my Changpa friends would stay in the hostel or with relatives in Leh…

S: This education provides them with new opportunities but prevents them from learning any of the skills required to be a Changpa. I remember a close Changpa friend who grew up in Leh. Once, when we were visiting his rebo, he was helping shear the goat and sheep. He had very little experience in this. The animals were very miserable and he ended up hurting some of them.

A: So, my friends will never be able to herd livestock even if they want to?

S: I don't know. This is the first generation being educated outside the community.

A: This means that it is possible that there might be no Changpas in the near future if the youth are not learning the skills and acquiring the necessary knowledge?

S: It is possible, if we try some innovative approaches, such as nomadic schools that move with the Changpas, allowing students to access education while also learning the skills needed to be a Changpa. If not, the Changpas will probably suffer the same fate as other communities in Ladakh, where knowledge and skills are being lost as the next generation finds other livelihoods.

A: That's a scary thought.

An apricot seller in Leh Market

One Step Forward and Back

Nidhi Dhingra

Once isolated from the rest of the world, today, the Main Bazaar Road in Leh has a buzz not unlike that of Manali, with tourists and locals rubbing shoulders and commercial establishments vying for attention. Just off it, archival photographs in the Central Asian Museum conjure up images of Leh City and the Ladakh that once was—making one imagine the dance its people must have danced, taking a step forward and then backward, over decades and generations, bringing them to where they are today.

'A lot has changed, yes,' says Tsewang Dolma, a programme lead at the Eicher Group Foundation from Matho Village. 'The changes startle those who return to Ladakh after a long gap. We've lived here through the changes, so it's not startling for us.'

Distance offers a broader perspective. Seen from an aeroplane, the bird's eye view of Ladakh is at once awe-inspiring and confounding. The landscape, characterised by miles upon miles of barren rugged ranges, underlines the challenge of merely sustaining human life in this formidable topography and altitude. And yet—incredibly so—the seemingly unending waves of peaks enfold within them a richness in life, colour and culture wildly contrasting with their swathes of brown. 'Ladakhis rarely ever leave Ladakh. They may go out to study or work briefly, but they always come back,' thirty-year-old Tsering Dolkar, a programme coordinator, tells us. Sporting slim fit jeans with a shirt fashionably tucked in on one side, and a pair of sunglasses resting on her head, she was dressed like any other GenZ from a metro city. While her family originally hails from Takmachik, a village in western Ladakh, Dolkar was born and raised in Leh.

It's incredible that this land has held on to its people despite its testing climes, where the winter temperatures plummet to a numbing -40 degrees and snowfields cut off months of access. The people of Ladakh have, for generations, powered through its many challenges and have found ways to grow with it.

Varied interactions over the next few days with locals from different walks of life allowed a glimpse beyond the city's easy-to-get-lost-in touristy garb. All conversations led to the same cross-section—of a robust culture built on the indomitable spirit of the locals and their utmost regard for nature. One by one the layers unpeeled revealing a self-sustaining Ladakh of the past, where sustainability was woven into every aspect of life—rather, seen as 'the only way to live'—building a foundation and upholding the ever-changing socio-economic-cultural landscape of the region. Thereon, with new eyes we looked closely for the Ladakh we'd come searching for.

***

In the old town of Leh, quaint mud structures stand out amidst concrete buildings. A climb up to LAMO (Ladakh Arts and Media Organisation), below Leh Palace, reveals the ingenious usage of space and material in this traditional method of construction—a response to the region's limited accessibility. The resident guide explains how the use of locally-available materials—mud, sand, poplar and willow—ensure that no time or labour is lost in transportation especially given the six-month window of inhospitable weather. Also, earth and wood are effective insulators, perfect for the region's extreme climatic contrasts.

In the layout, the most-used room, i.e., the kitchen, faces south for maximum sunlight and has a huge window. The bedroom is next to it so that heat generated from cooking can add to its warmth at night. A source informed us, 'Used to its potential, this building technique would keep the indoors at a comfortable 200 degrees celsius throughout the year.' Often, even with the recent addition of flush toilets, a dechod or a dry compost toilet stands close to the main structure. A perceptive solution to managing human waste sustainably in the water-stressed landscape, traditionally, it also gave rich compost for fertilising the local fields, vegetable and flower gardens. 'The chhurpon system, an age-old system of rotational water-sharing, enabled the farmers of Ladakh to convert patches of semi-arid land to rich, cultivated fields,' Tashi Morup, the projects director at LAMO enlightens us. 'Even while the land under agriculture has reduced over time, the chhurpon system is still used in most interior villages.'

Using traditional wood-and-stone water mills called rantaks, energy from fast-flowing streams has been used for grinding grains—barley, millet, buckwheat, wheat—for centuries. 'Though their importance has diminished with the availability of mill flour, the taste of the rantak-ground flour remains unmatched,' a local shares proudly. Sampling local food, we learnt how the limited availability of ingredients has brought about a distinct Ladakhi cuisine, with easy-to-make, simple, fuel-efficient preparations—

A weaver woman at work in LAMO

At Lamchung Tsepail's workshop in Likir

cooked to lend not just flavour but also the energy, vitality and warmth essential for these climes. 'In Ladakh,' Tsewang Namgail, a researcher and biologist, informs us, 'nas or barley has been cultivated as the central food grain. A great source of fibre, it is often ground and roasted into ngamphe (roasted barley flour), occupying a core place in local activities. What is not turned into ngamphe is brewed into chhang, a fermented barley beer, pale-yellow and bubbly when fresh.'

Namgail continues, 'Until the 1970s, the tradition of having endless cups of gurgur cha or butter tea throughout the day was a symbol of Ladakhiness.' More soup-like than tea, the traditional recipe had salt and fresh yak butter churned with a concentrate of a special Tibetan variety of tea, with water and milk. 'The butter gives energy and warmth to the body, preventing flaky skin from cold dry winds; and the salt helps absorb excess water from the body to reduce thirst in the dry climate. It is the perfect hydrating beverage for the dry climate of Ladakh, and the first thing to be served to guests.'

'The name gur gur cha comes from the sound made by the traditional churner (dongmo): gur gur gur, as the ingredients are blended in,' explains Muzammil Hussain from Kargil. While fresh yak butter has now vastly been replaced with Amul, and the preparation simplified, making gur gur cha is still a daily ritual in most households.

The dongmos in Ladakhi kitchens—varying in vintage from the exquisitely-carved and brass-fitted wooden ones to the rather uncharacteristic plastic ones—are now retained more for sentiment than for use. 'I don't like butter tea much myself, but I make it often for my parents,' Dolkar tells us over a cup of this unique beverage. 'They have it every day.' Namgail adds, 'The skyu made of wheat or barley dumplings, cooked with fresh vegetables or meat, is packed with nutrition and calories and is popular across the region, both with locals and tourists alike. As is paba, made with roasted barley (ngamphey) flour, turtle beans, wheat flour, brown peas, and lentils.'

Despite the host of multi-cuisine options available in bigger cities and towns today, establishments offering traditional fare hold their own—drawing, and often even run by, youngsters with an intent to share their food with the world. 'Nomadic pastoralism was once practised across a wider territory in Ladakh and preceded agriculture,' Tara Sharma, a cultural specialist, points out. 'Wool was produced primarily for trade where it was bartered for essentials such as grain across a network of trade routes; in addition to being consumed for the herders' own needs.'

The spinning of wool, once a part of the identity of a Ladakhi villager, comes from the unspoken tradition of using naturally available resources efficiently. A weaver woman casually shares: 'The sheep were there, producing wool, so putting that wool to use was simply a part of life.' Today, supported by organisations such as Jungwa Foundation and Looms of Ladakh, the weaving industry is witnessing a much-needed revival. Several craftspeople have returned to their family occupation with a renewed spirit. The identifying Ladakhi garment, a woollen robe called goncha, woven from handspun wool, continues to be the most practical and reliable winter wear for Ladakhi villagers; often seen sharing space with jackets and sweaters in shop windows.

The topical character of Ladakh permeates its arts and culture as well. Likir, the most significant potters' village of Ladakh, came to

Ladakh Arts and Media Organisation in old town of Leh

Display centre at Chilling, selling famed brass and copperware

be assigned its role of pottery-making by the ruling Namgyal kings of Ladakh (in the fourteenth century), owing to the availability of natural clay and sand deposits in its environs. Similarly, in the sixteenth century, Newari metalsmiths from Nepal were granted land at the present site of Chilling owing to rich deposits of alluvial gold and copper found in the Zanskar river (zang is Tibetan for copper, and skar is valley) during that time. Today, Likir and Chilling are garnering awareness and interest of both local authorities and outsiders, giving a boost to the families persevering with these traditional crafts.

'Conical, backpack baskets called tSepo have for centuries served as an economic lifeline for the locals,' conservationist Sonam Wangchuk tells us. Hand-woven out of willow twigs and a locally available grass known as ichibkang, they are used for carrying everything: from firewood to vegetables, manure to animal feed, and even babies! Fading out under the influx of plastic, they are now being revived with targeted conservation efforts in Nubra. 'Jabro, the most popular folk dance of Ladakh, came into existence as a way to beat the cold (jab is "feet" and ro is "to warm"),' a local woman explains. In the highlands of Changthang, their feet freezing from the icy winds, the nomadic Changpas would light a fire and break into a foot-tapping dance around it, to warm themselves up. Soon it became an integral part of their lives, performed by both men and women on all festive occasions; best seen at the Losar celebrations. The dance is performed wearing warm, knee-length boots locally known as paabu, made from wool, cloth, and felt; and is performed by communities across Ladakh today.

Each of the conversations shed light on how the traditional Ladakhi way of life echoed its surrounding landscape. With the passage of time and exposure to the outside world, while the manner of interaction with the land has found a new expression, the direction of change is not linear but a navigation of the new with the old. That said, the way forward is backward—in a more conscious shift to engaging with the traditional practices in a manner prudent and pertinent to suit the changing times.[1]

1 From a research trip to Leh to document the region's intangible cultural practices, for Eicher Goodearth Foundation.

Kargil beyond the War

Nidhi Dhingra

'While I was studying and working outside Ladakh—in Pune and Delhi—the people there would keep questioning my identity, asking questions like: Where is Kargil? Are you from Pakistan? Do you need a visa to go there? Very strange questions!' Muzammil Hussain, a Ladakhi and co-founder of Roots Ladakh, shares with indignation. 'And those questions used to really bother me! Then, I realised that as an outsider, you only consume what you are shown. Kargil was heavily televised during the 1999 War, so people had only that image of it. While, for me, it was home. I had the best memories of growing up in Kargil—hiking and trekking in its beautiful valleys in summers, and playing in its endless snowfields in the carefree, downtime months of winter.'

The subject of identity has long plagued the Kargilis, stemming from a misrepresentation of the region. Its people were treated as outsiders and often viewed with suspicion when it came to their loyalty to the country (up until the war in 1999). 'It's very interesting,' remarks Muzammil, 'that living on the frontier we have to always keep proving our integrity, whereas somebody sitting in the plains can talk about being patriotic without really knowing what it means.'

Munshi Aziz Bhat & Sons on a usual day at the Sarai in Kargil in 1945 A.D.

Credits: Munshi Aziz Bhat Museum, Kargil (www.kargilmuseum.org)

Not only that—sandwiched between Kashmir and Leh, the local identity of Kargilis has often been wrongly construed. Until October 2019, when Ladakh was declared a Union Territory, 'due to religious affinity, the Shi'a-majority Kargili Muslims were often subsumed under a general pan-Kashmiri Sunni–Muslim umbrella.'

While in actuality, 'despite conversion to Islam, the Muslims of Kargil continue to share cultural affinities with the wider Trans-Himalayan region that stretches from Baltistan in the west to the Tibetan plateau in the east. They speak a dialect of classical Tibetan, dress in gonchas (woollen robes), share dietary habits with barley as the staple, drink butter tea, construct flat-roofed mudbrick houses and celebrate the same seasonal festivals, albeit modified to incorporate religious injunctions. Unfortunately, though, Kargil has tended to be relatively invisible or neglected in popular and scholarly representations of Ladakh as well.'[1]

Thus, for the Kargilis, there has always been a need to assert both their Indian as well as Ladakhi identity to the people of their own country. Not surprising that, for many locals, this translated into a lack of self-esteem in their regional and cultural roots. The work of cultural activists in Kargil, pioneered by Muzammil Hussain, can be seen as an attempt to rectify this. To churn the wheel of 'cultural consciousness that spills beyond the politics of identity to an emotionally and intellectually-charged process of self-definition'[1]—for the Kargilis to be known, recognised and respected on their own terms. For Muzammil, the idea of building Roots Ladakh, a sustainable tourism organisation promoting Kargil, was not just a bid to change the popular narrative of Kargil

---

1 Gupta, Radhika. (2013), The Importance of Being Ladakhi: Affect and Artifice in Kargil, HIMALAYA 32-1.

but also to own with pride the heritage of his own family that he stumbled upon, quite by chance! 'One summer when I came home for my vacation, in 2002 or 2003, I went to my paternal uncle's house, and the living room had these antique-looking things lined up. On inquiring, I learned that our family had a sarai (an inn for travellers), and these were all items recovered from there. Forget knowing that we owned a sarai, I didn't even know what a sarai was!'

He goes on, 'From there, as if the floodgates had opened, the rich history of my family as well as of Kargil started to unfold for me, fascinating me every step of the way.' Originally Kashmiri Brahmins from Kishtwar, Muzammil's family, like many others, had converted to Islam under the influence of revolutionaries during the Mughal period but retained their last name: Bhat. Muzammil Hussain's great–great-grandfather, Khoja Rasool Bhat, a record keeper with Maharaja Pratap Singh of the Jammu and Kashmir government, was a well-known figure. As was his son, Munshi Aziz Bhat, who got his father's job after his passing. Born in Leh in 1866, Munshi Aziz married four women, two Buddhists, and two Muslims, and had fifteen children in all—the different faiths housed under one roof signifying the composite culture and communal harmony in Kargil.

It was a time when trading on the Silk Route was the most coveted business. 'Over time, the Route had expanded to become a multi-directional, trans-continental thoroughfare for traffic on horseback, donkey, mule, yak and foot, trading every possible item of daily as well as luxury use. Goods were dispatched from Asia to several ports and towns in Africa, Europe, and the Americas, bartering produce for manufactured items, between traders from all over the world. Later, with the influence of the East India

Company and Christian missionaries, goods began to be traded in money and silver coins.'[2]

Kargil, with its strategic location, had developed into one of the key feeder routes for the trade. Placed equidistant from Kashmir, Baltistan (in Pakistan), Zanskar and Leh, all within a radius of 180–200 km, it was said that 'all the roads lead to Kargil'. In fact, the name Kargil itself is derived from the word 'garkill', meaning 'a place to stop from all directions'. True to its name, it was an important stop on the Treaty Road from Srinagar to Leh and Central Asia.

It was in this charged environment that Munshi Aziz quit his secure job as a patwari or village accountant for the revenue department, to try his luck in business. Based on credit and trust, trading on the Silk Route was for the elite, since goods sent over long distances sans any communication brought back returns only after months. At that time, it was run and controlled in Ladakh solely by Punjabis and Hoshiarpurias. No one locally had the capital to be part of it—until Munshi Aziz came to prominence.

He started out as a rival to his competitors but soon joined them to establish himself as a trader in Kargil. Partnering with a Sikh merchant, Sardar Kant Singh, he started a retail-wholesale shop with a capital of 6,000 silver coins (the equivalent of Rs 6 lakhs today) and by the end of the year had made a profit of Rs 9,000. In 1920, he established his trading business with his two older sons and a cousin, calling it 'Munshi Aziz Bhat & Sons.'[2]

Imported from Europe and Central Asia, the shop sold textiles, carpets, toiletries, stationery, cosmetics, medicines, spices and shoe

2 Hussain, Muzammil. (2013), The Last Great Silk Route Trader Of India, The Indian Memory Project, - https://www.indianmemoryproject.com/114/.

Museum of Memories, Hundurman, Kargil

Credits: Roots Ladakh

Old town of Leh characterised by a syncretic culture, with a gurdwara, mosque and monastery within a stone's throw

Credits: Muzzamil Hussain

polish (considered a luxury item). It also sold atypical items such as horse and camel accessories, catering to the large demand for decorating these four-legged vehicles regarded as a status symbol (much like cars today). Stocking such a varied range of goods in a landscape of barren high mountains, with no paved roads or motor vehicles, was indeed no small feat. Once established in business, Munshi Aziz built the first-ever inn in Kargil for Central Asian traders, called the Aziz Bhat Sarai. Built in 1920, the three-storey square building still stands by the banks of the River Suru in the old Caravan Bazaar. The Sarai was the main hub of activities, a depot for goods meant for all directions, including the Tibet, India and Baltistan routes, and housed Bhat's seven shops. Known far and wide for its variety of goods, it had become part of the local folklore: one could even find birds' milk at the Munshi Aziz Bhat Sarai.[3]

Munshi Aziz had become one of the most influential people in the whole of Ladakh and Baltistan wizarat. As a petition writer for the Maharaja, he had networked with princes, kings and high-ranking officials from all across the world, including the Moravian missionaries and East India Company officials who frequented the town for business and strategic concerns. He knew English, was literate and fair in his dealings, thus earning a reputation of a man with integrity. 'I can just imagine the life of my great grandfather,' Muzammil says, wistfully. 'The kind of people he would have met and interacted with—missionaries, spies, military, traders—coming all the way from Yarkand, Khotan and Samarkand. My grandmother would talk about Central Asians, coming to Kargil with their ware; and the specially designed yurt-like tents that the would trade for rice and other essentials with the local traders.'

---

3 Hussain, Muzammil. (2013), The Last Great Silk Route Trader Of India, The Indian Memory Project, - https://www.indianmemoryproject.com/114/.

The Silk Route trade saw its last days during the Partition of India, following which, all the major trade routes between India and Pakistan, as well as businesses along it, were forced to shut down. Munshi Aziz Bhat Sarai met with a similar fate. Thereon, the Munshi family left the Silk Route trade, and most of its members either joined politics or government service. The Sarai remained locked—and the cultural legacy was forgotten—for almost half a century before the chance discovery prompted efforts that (on the persuasion of a foreign researcher, Jaqueline Fewkes) culminated in the establishment of a museum.

'Opened in 2004, the Munshi Aziz Bhat Museum for Silk Route and Central Asian Trade is an endeavour of Gulzar Hussain Munshi and Ajaz Hussain Munshi (Muzammil's paternal uncles) to collect, preserve and display objects circulated along the trade routes between Ladakh and Yarkand and other material relics of everyday life that are no longer easily found or used'[4], writes Radhika Gupta. Named after their grandfather, the museum displays a variety of artefacts— horse saddles, tapestries, utensils, coins, old manuscripts and photographs, costumes, and jewellery—that give a rare glimpse into the Indian and central Asian business culture of the 19th and early 20th centuries.'

***

'In the larger scheme, Kargil has been a very important part of history, and yet, when people think of it, they only think of the war,' Muzammil continues. 'As a thriving trade town, not just goods but ideas were also exchanged here. Different religions, concepts and cultures have travelled through the region and mingled. It is thus that Kargil today is home to at least six different ethnicities

---

4 Gupta, Radhika. (2013), The Importance of Being Ladakhi: Affect and Artifice in Kargil, HIMALAYA 32-1.

of people. There's the local Purigi community (Kargil's original settlers); Baltis from Baltistan (now in Pakistan); Kashmiris, like us, who have integrated into the local culture for generations; Brokpas from Aryan Valley, Shina in Drass, Boto in the Nindum Valley as well as the Hoshiarpuri Punjabis mostly living in the main town of Kargil. This diverse mix of cultures is now translated into the Kargili food, language, way of dressing and a lot of other customs.'

For Muzammil, on returning to Kargil in 2013, the work for building Roots Ladakh, along with his brother, Tafazzul (the co-founder of Roots), began with an entire year just spent on local research. 'We were trying to understand our own place, to be able to promote it in a different light. We wanted to change the modern-day travellers' outlook to Kargil where it was seen only as a one-night destination. There were two major challenges—the complete lack of information on the region, and the absence of skilled resources. For the first three or four years, my brother and I were doing every single thing ourselves. The biggest surprise was the positive reception of the idea by the locals. Even as they were apprehensive of outsiders' interest in their everyday lives and culture, they embraced our attempts to rewrite the [un] popular narrative; coming forward with a keenness to learn more about their own cultural and regional identity that most had lost touch with.' Soon enough, Roots Ladakh became a name almost synonymous with the region, and a local brand for tourism in Kargil. 'With Roots, one of the best experiences on offer is the Himalayan Brown Bear experience. And what, I feel, should get more limelight is trekking, especially in Suru Valley where routes are still preserved in their raw, natural form, unlike other parts of Ladakh where road construction has obliterated them. With Nun and Kun—the two highest peaks in the Zanskar range—Suru Valley is also great for climbing and mountaineering.'

Muzammil goes on, with pride, 'In general, Kargil is an offbeat, lesser-known place where you can still find quaint locations. It also has very interesting local festivals, like the Mamani and Bono nah, for visitors to experience. Our greatest achievement, without doubt, has been the revival of pride in identity among the locals. At a micro level, whether you're a Balti, Shina, Brokpa or a Purigi, the cultural identities are slowly getting embraced again. The customs and traditions that were left behind are now being rediscovered.'

I asked him if Kargil was safe to visit, and pat came the reply: 'It's very surprising that even twenty years after the war, people still ask that question. It says a lot about the impression that one event has made. I think it's safer than travelling in Delhi or any other big city, where there are more unpredictable elements. Moreover, if people can travel to Kashmir in such big numbers, where the situation is often volatile and unpredictable, I don't see why people can't visit Kargil.'

From an interview with Muzammil Hussain, the co-founder of Roots Ladakh (https://rootsladakh.com/) and references from the Munshi Aziz Bhat Museum of Central Asian & Kargil Trade Artefacts, Kargil (https://kargilmuseum.org/)

Taking Pashmina to Paris

Manasi Chokshi

'You know, the winters here are so cold, that if you happen to step outside with freshly washed hair, it will freeze, like icicles,' laughs Kunzes Angmo, the co-founder of Lehvallee, a socially responsible and organic brand of handmade textiles based in Leh. 'But I love the cold winters of Ladakh. I was very happy to be back in Ladakh to live amidst the mountains and rivers. I guess one appreciates the beautiful landscape only after living away from home.'

The retail showroom, Lehvallee, is situated at the junction of the Fort Road and Tukcha Main Road, in Lakrook Hotel in Leh, and its workshop is based in Choglamsar. The showroom has a collection of beautiful shawls, handbags, pouches, upholstery, and so on, made in Pashmina wool, yak wool and sheep wool, in soothing and muted tones of pastel blues, oranges, pinks and greys, with contemporary patterns and designs. The airy and minimal showroom puts you at ease the moment you step in. Sitting in her showroom, Kunzes continues: 'Back in 2012, my sister Sonam already had a project called "Young Doll". Having worked in the media industry and now living and working in France, she had Lehvallee in mind for a long time. The weaver from the workshop, she was our first employee. She and I started exploring the world

Credits: Subin Selva

of textiles from a small place in Leh. It was on the third floor, a big hall, where we set up two or three looms. Honestly, with my degree in Chemistry from Delhi University, I was very reluctant to venture into this. But, when I touched and felt the first fabric I made, it felt so good, so fulfilling. Then there was no turning back. We applied for a PMEGP (Prime Minister's Employment Generation Programme) loan of 25 lakhs. The PMEGP is an initiative by the Government of India's Ministry of Micro, Small and Medium Enterprises. And that is how Lehvallee began in 2017.'

The Angmo sisters began by building their workshop at Choglamsar. The simple and efficient workshop building sits against the beautiful backdrop of the Ladakh Dharma centre and the Ladakh mountain range. It is a textile manufacturing unit with facilities to spin, dye, weave, design and stitch. The responsibilities are shared: Kunzes takes care of the production and operation at the workshop and sales at the store in Leh, while Sonam looks after the post manufacturing responsibilities like communications, business development, store design, online sale, graphics, and so on, from the city of Nantes in France.

'I was brought up in a house along the Indus. In the winters the river would freeze, and we could see the water flowing under the ice. That little place in my home backyard continues to be my favourite spot, but the river is drying up. I have heard the migration of fishes for breeding is also affected. Ecologically, we are in a highly sensitive zone. But what to do? The economy of Ladakh largely relies on tourism. The population that visits Ladakh in these few months, from June to September, surpasses the population of Ladakh. The water consumption is being affected. Ladakhis use less water, but tourists and tourist activity require more water. Everyone here will tell you that we want sustainable tourism, but no one will be telling you how to achieve that. And they probably would not be ready to follow a sustainable lifestyle either. Tourism is not a sustainable option: in terms of economy and ecology both.

'Keeping all this in mind, we try creating products that are organic and timeless; something that can be used over the years and can eventually go back to the earth. We try to have a system where zero chemicals are used in the manufacturing of the products. All colours are natural and completely organic. We create colours from onion skins, walnut shells, marigold flowers, indigo (sourced from Jaipur as it doesn't grow here) majishta (Indian madder). We also source some insect-based dyes like Cochineal. This cannot be found in India. We source it from France. This is where my expertise in Chemistry comes into play. Since I manage the complete production from Ladakh, I hardly get any time to experiment with colours and dyes. My dream is to run a laboratory dedicated completely to dyes and colours. We feel that our business should be socially responsible and contemporise the traditional weaves to make it accessible to a wider spectrum of people. Only then the traditional fabrics and weaves will be revived and valued.'

The process of making a traditional Ladakhi wool fabric begins with sourcing, cleaning and spinning the yarn. The nomadic tribes from the region of Changthang are popular for rearing the Changthangi goats for Pashmina—a fine quality of wool that yields the warmest and thinnest woollen textile. The Pashmina thread from these goats is delicate and requires skilled labour, which Ladakhi women are experts at. Kunzes reminisces, 'I have seen my grandma hand-spinning yarn. In the winters, two or three ladies would sit in the sun or around a bukhari, chit-chatting and spinning with their hands. The hands would move in sync with the flow of the conversations. Thus, spinning is part of all households.'

Like the Pashmina is yielded from Changthangi goats, the yaks are reared in the Nubra region for yak wool. This quality of yak wool is thicker and warmer than the Pashmina. There are co-operative societies in Leh that source and clean the yarn and roll it into yarn balls. These yarn balls are then converted into hangs that are dyed and dried. The dyed and dried yarns are then woven on looms. Out of all these processes, weaving is the process that continues even through the winters. 'Currently, we have employed around a hundred women,' says Kunzes, elaborating the ecologically and socially conscious ideologies of the brand, 'for spinning, dyeing and weaving. This makes them financially and socially independent. Recently, there has been government support: they offer training workshops and looms for the women, and this also has been successful.'

One of the other primary ideas of the brand is to build timeless and sustainable relationships with their customers. Citing an example, Kunzes says, 'I have a customer from southern India who loves and visits Ladakh very often. During each trip, she visits us and buys many gifts and mementos. On one of the trips, she bought a shawl for her mother. On her next trip to Ladakh, she mentioned to me that her mother has a habit of returning all gifts she buys for her, but the shawl from Lehvallee she refuses to part with. So, you know, that is the kind of timelessness and warmth we are trying to aim at.

'The store receives all kinds of customers; foreign and Indian both. But, due to the similar climatic conditions, foreign tourists relate more with our products. Pashmina or Cashmere is very popular amongst European travellers. Since our weave designers are from London, France, etc., the designs also appeal to the foreign clientele. The Indian tourist belongs to a relatively warmer region. They compensate by buying smaller items like pouches, handbags and things like that. To facilitate their demands, we also keep products made from yarns from Ludhiana—basically fabric that is dyed, designed and tailored by us; but the yarn is handspun from Ludhiana. These are cheaper and comparatively less warm than the Pashmina and yak wool.'

The sisters wish to expand their brand in multiple ways. Socially, they want to work directly with the nomads for the yarn, set up a trust, adopt villages, set up clusters and much more. To reach a still wider audience, they wish to expand their business in India and France, physically and virtually. The passion towards this runs so deep that Sonam has even moved to a larger city in France, and closer to Paris for better business prospects. Sonam and Kunzes are building a brand whose fundamental philosophy is to create a timeless and selfless relationship with the environment and people, locally and globally. Their rootedness in Ladakhi tradition and international exposure is helping them convert a local artefact into a product of international standard. Armed with high values, the Angmo sisters are in a persistent and passionate pursuit of establishing an identity for Ladakh on the map of India and the world.

They are a part of the revival journey that is ecologically and socially responsible—the one that revives the traditional craft of Ladakhi textiles, based in the homeland of Ladakh, and creates products that appeal to people from across the world.

Local Learnings

Riddhima Khedkar

'....I first visited Ladakh for a music confluence in 2010, and I simply fell in love with the place. It was the people, the culture, the landscape, the architecture, the pristine beauty, just everything! I visited again in 2011, just as I was starting my undergraduate thesis research. I stayed here for four months and did my research work. My thesis research topic was "Sacred Architecture in Public Spaces of Ladakh". I was inquiring into how the sacred comes out of the public realm. How do people use public spaces?'

Purnima Das is an enthusiastic young architect who moved her base to Leh in 2017. She works there for nine months of the year, and the remaining three months, when the city is non-functional on account of heavy winters, she is either back home spending quality time with her family, pursuing her hobbies or taking up small-scale projects.

Facts state that Ladakh is one of the coldest places on the planet (where the residents don't have any fuel to heat their houses). Historically linked with the Silk Route connecting the Indian subcontinent with the north Karakoram ranges, showcasing South and East Asian socio-cultural influences, the region

Credits: Author

exhibits a robust Buddhist culture with traces of Hinduism and Islam. Since the region's inception, the structures have been climate- and earthquake-sensitive, using locally available materials and abundant solar energy to make ends meet. The architecture includes monasteries, gompas, royal palaces, cave temples and old houses in the region's rural parts. In the 1970s, when the region opened for tourism, it attracted an increasing number of travellers because of its landscape, heritage, culture, tradition, serene environment, etc.

Today, Ladakh has become more of a tourist hub than a military or economy centre. One sees tourists ranging from intellectuals to leisure travellers to honeymooners to campers to anybody and everybody. Because of such a boom in tourism, globalisation genuinely began in the region. With globalisation comes modern approaches and heavy infrastructural developments. The Vision 2050 for Union Territory of Ladakh terms these developments as Smart Infrastructure along with the addition of integrated growth for creating hubs of development, urbanisation and economy with the aid of community, cluster and connectivity. Additionally, new initiatives and social groups, such as women-run co-operative/s, LEDeG (Ladakh Ecological Development Group), etc., have been initiated to uplift the preservation of Ladakh's traditional culture and values. These new initiatives and social groups are said to weave a new sustainable story of Ladakh into the modern world.

Architects such as Suril Patel and Faiza Khan of Field Architects, and Bogadhi Sandeep of Earthling, to name a few, are trying hard to bring about gradual yet deep-seated change by experimenting with local materials to create new strategic developments in the form of a critical regionalist approach. During one of Purnima's stays in Leh, she recalls seeing a lot of cement buildings with a considerable amount of HVAC (Heating Ventilation Air Conditioning) trying to keep the spaces warm. She says, '….I feel all the materials are coming in the city (in Leh) because of the want. There is demand and supply for modern materials such as cement and concrete. There is a lack of education and awareness, which needs to change soon. Thorough changes, such as having a sincere discussion and a conscious choice to retain the vernacular factor of this region, are a must.'

She further says, 'It's a difficult choice, and a challenge, to be modern and local simultaneously. It involves thinking out of the box, inventing a few things, experimenting, and having to fail. We do not want to fail at anything. But that's my outlook. We don't want to fail in our endeavours, which makes us very careful and scared to do anything new.' Modern day materials such as cement and concrete are being used extensively in regions conducive to local materials like mud, adobe and stone. With the age of modernisation, the idea of sustainability and vernacularity has taken a backseat, or at least the approach has become more hybrid. People construct the foundation using cement with a skeletal mud structure or ornamental wooden element cladding on an RCC (Reinforced Cement Concrete) frame structure, which is then called a 'local structure'.

After completing her bachelor's in architecture from the Centre of Environmental Planning and Technology (CEPT), Ahmedabad, Purnima did not visit Ladakh for the longest time. In 2017, she decided to revisit Ladakh because she missed the place, and she established her firm Hearth Creations by taking on her first passion project. Little did she know that this would be a challenging ride as Ladakh is a remote place—but, at the same time, one where humanity is advancing, albeit not at the pace of the technologically driven world we all live in. She spoke to many people around; she had to source her labourers from outside the region as the locals were labourers only if they were trying to build something by themselves.

She then talks about how she worked on her first project in Ladakh, an ancient house. The owners took down the house as it had no income. The owners did not imagine it would be financially viable. After a lot of convincing, she persuaded them to give her the house on a lease. She then started work on restoring the house. Since the house was ancient, she started by replacing the dummas (a Ladakhi term used for the primary beams in a structure, in this case the house), which was the main body of work for the project. '… the idea here was to set an example through this project and get it in the running mode so that the people around and the owners themselves could figure out that these types of spaces can generate a financial bulk amount resulting in the achievement of a formal business model.'

Comparing the developments that happened in the pre- and post-2017, Purnima sees a lot of old houses using adaptive reuse as a significant way forward now. She observes that many people have started using local architecture to build new forms. She is an inspiration for setting an example by taking a risk and executing a commendable task that changed Leh's socio-cultural and physical landscape. But she is also disheartened to know that the house was demolished and turned into a shopping complex later. At the same time, she is glad that many people are learning from this, and one can see change taking place. '….I have been to the places built recently, and very frankly, the people there have told me that my work inspires this (the change). I mean, it is not about me; it is about the landscape changing, going back to where it was. I do

Credits: Jiten Desai

Credits: Jiten Desai

hope that they take it forward. Through this project, I feel that a bit of my aim has been taken care of. But I also see many people constructing mindlessly with cement and stuff.'

She then talks about her next project, where her aim is restoration and doing something not seen or done in Leh—she will be working on a project made totally out of waste. Her idea of waste is not plastic or glass bottles but the waste that one finds in scrapyards, which is more significant. Who would have imagined that a place like Ladakh would have scrapyards! The demolition of old houses generated a lot of waste. She used old house pillars and beams, old mud blocks and rafters, vehicle parts, anything and everything found in the scrapyards, and local materials such as stone and mud to create this large space.

Her motive is to preserve the land and keep it as pristine as possible so that when one leaves it, it returns to itself. About 40 per cent of the project is complete, a crucial bit and the larger module. While she plans to finish the remaining 60 per cent in the following year, she claims to have used only about half a bag of cement and structured a foundation with used rubber tires from trucks.

Like Purnima's projects, these projects go on to serve as a demonstrative process for locals to identify resources around them and rework on ideas for developing sensible and logical structural solutions that can undergo the harsh and extreme climatic conditions throughout the year. Since the architecture is in line with the ecology, the building needs to be more in line with economical, ecological and empathetically designed or restored structures. This seems to have been slowly on the decline due to changing lifestyles and professions and users being the new-age travellers whose ideas and aspirations are futuristic, technology-based and driven by wants and needs. This creates further divide where globalisation and modernisation take precedence over vernacularity and regionalism.

Although home to many heritage sites, a lot of the local structures are in need of conservation; changing weather patterns with bouts of extreme climatic spells, ignorance, thirst for fast-paced modernisation and developments using RCC have led to the negligence of heritage sites and further resulted in taking down the sites because of economic issues. If one took a critical regionalist approach, using local materials with a modern twist—keeping in mind the limitations as well as the scope of experimentation—the structures could be both humble and powerful, compared to the new-age, environmentally unfriendly RCC structures.

This approach would be looked at as a sensitive way of preserving the land, contributing to reduce the carbon footprint generated by non-local materials such as cement and keeping the land pristine and unharmed. So that when one leaves, it is returned to itself, having aged beautifully and gracefully with time for the eco-cultural future.

The architectural design language of Ladakh is very intergenerational and relies mainly on earth, stone and wood, the roots of which have originated from Tibet and Central Asia, which have similar climate and resources. In such regions, the local materials and their materiality form the crux of the structure. Local Ladakhi architecture design is simple and pure. The design evolves from the available resources and the surrounding landscape.

Practising in this region, as compared to a metropolitan city, allows designers to touch upon aspects such as experience, materials, crafts, ecology, sociology and the environment. Although it is a slow process, but it is satisfyingly rewarding in the end. It allows the designer to experiment, evaluate and identify throughout the process of construction and constantly evolve to create better and locally modern solutions.

Frankly, a job like this is a tough one, where a single project can take up to two to four years, or even more, for completion. Based on the ground reality at source and the financial strength of the client, some projects remain as passion projects on paper due to unforeseen circumstances. Not to forget that the remuneration received is hardly any as compared to the inspiration that the designers serve to the community at large. As much as the architectural profession is highly niche and becomes more and more lucrative by the day, designers working in remote regions such as Ladakh should be held in high esteem for striving hard to give back to the community through what they've learnt in the process of adapting, evolving and reviving themselves as designers each day.

The Healing Hot Springs of Ladakh

Jigmet Lhazes

Amchi Tsewang Rigzen, of Merak village, in the Changthang region of Ladakh, speaks of the hot springs in Ladakh as a healing hotspot in the Sowa Rigpa system of medicine. He is one of the very well-known practitioners of the Buddhist healing system. He calmly sits with a group of people in his tent who are his patients and residents of the village. Amchi, a Mongolian word that means medicine practitioner, treats his patients in a tent as the others discuss politics over the Indo–China border issues.

'The hot spring of Demchok has existed since the formation of the Trans-Himalayan region. Earlier, two generations ago, this hot spring was located at the banks of River Demchok in China, somewhere in shrubby vegetation,' says Amchi Urgain, a young man sitting on a chair.

He gets up to leave as his patients have finished the bath therapy in the spring. Hot springs—a formation of coal and sulphur, the hydrothermal area where bubbling hot water rises from the earth's crust. Sowa Rigpa is a traditional medicine system that understands and utilises the medicinal properties of the hot springs.

The Demchok hot spring is located in Demchok village, at the border of India and China, in the Changthang area of Ladakh. Earlier a big town, the Chinese occupied half of its area. After the war, the Demchok river divided the two countries, leaving the hot spring to India.

Amchi Tsewang, yet another of the group, has returned from meditation. 'Demchok hot spring is very special in the valley. It is blissful. Those who come here to have their bath therapy must have a pure mind and faith. The hot springs are located on a plateau on the bank of the river. The breast, eyes, stomach, head, knees and waist, the form of the spring determines its identity. The springs collectively flow in the bathrooms built for the patients to have the therapy near the residential camps.'

Amchi Urgain believes, 'The special character of Demchok hot spring is that it is beneficial for every disease; from a general spring to specialised ones for contagious disease, Bad-Kan diseases, stomach disease, eye disease, and breast disease. It could be a future centre for geo-medical tourism!' In Sowa Rigpa, the diseases are classified based on cold-natured and hot-natured. Ladakhi people are dependent on Sowa Rigpa practitioners for chronic diseases to have hot spring therapy.

In Sowa Rigpa, there are five types of hot springs; and Ladakh is home to over a hundred spread across the regions of Changthang, Nubra, Zanskar and Sham. 'Except Demchok, I have not visited other hot springs,' says Amchi Urgain as he explains the process of bath therapy, 'First, one needs to have a bath at the spring, which is for infectious disease (contagious disease) for five minutes initially, and increase five minutes subsequently every day for the prescribed period. If the water is too hot, it affects blood pressure and can prove dangerous. People with high blood pressure normally avoid spring baths.'

Amchi Tsewang of Merak explains: 'Generally, people have therapy for the knee and waist. After that, people drink Badkan hot spring water as a medicinal drink. Specifically, nerve disorder and stroke are cured here. Each spring cures distinctly depending on water velocity and direction. Some at the backside of the body cure nerve disorders and spinal problems. Yet, another hot spring requires pouring the water on the body to evade stroke, and focuses individually on eyes, ears and breasts.'

Amchi Tashi Tsering, a well-known practitioner of Sowa Rigpa of Ladakh, is from the Tsaga village of Changthang. Arriving at our discussion, he says, 'I was at the forest collecting some herbs for the cure.' He explains, 'The bath therapy works as a catalyst with medicinal herbs for long-term acute illness.' The bath therapy method requires Amchi supervision by the Sowa Rigpa practitioners. Every year, all Amchis visit the springs with their patients twice, during spring and autumn.

As the villages and hot springs lie on the Indo–China border, their conservation becomes a matter of national importance. The cultural, geological and medicinal conservation benefits the Sowa Rigpa practitioners, tourists, the People of Ladakh and therefore India.

Statue of Maitreya Buddha in Disket Monastry, Nubra Valley

The Sacred Valley

Dr Sonam Wangchuk

Ladakh's harsh environment has fostered a vibrant cultural heritage, visible in every aspect of local life. It is not surprising to see significant influences of Tibet, Kashmir and other places, given the close ties that the region has historically had with its neighbours. However, what distinguishes Ladakh from other places is how these influences have blended to form a unique tradition linked to its 'sacred landscape': the natural landscape's sacred components, which have an effect on the community's way of life. It also refers to sacred mountain ranges and rock formations, lakes, springs, caves, hermitages, pastures and places of minerals. The Rongdo Gonbo (also known as the sacred valley of Mahakala), which attracts pilgrims every year on the fifteenth day of the fourth lunar month (Buddha Jayanti), is one such holy site in Ladakh.

The monk in charge leads some villagers there the day before to prepare for the rituals and provide refreshments for the pilgrims. When pilgrims arrive at the temple at the base of the mountain on which the Mahakala can be found, the residents of Rongdo provide them with food and refreshments. Over two decades ago, at around half past four in the morning, my brother-in-law and I arrived in Rongdo village to join the pilgrims. After almost thirty minutes of waiting, we were given butter tea and barley flour (tsampa or phey). We waited for almost an hour to see if more pilgrims would arrive, but none did. There were also a couple of villagers waiting to lead the pilgrims. One of them told us around half past five that it didn't seem like anyone was coming that year and told us to go on because the trail's beginning is steep and therefore hard to climb. They advised us to take it steady and to begin the walk gradually. Along with two guides, two pilgrims set off.

Rongdo Gonbo is also known as Pata Gonbo because the Tibetan letters 'Pa' and 'Ta' spontaneously emerged on the surface of a mountain above the village, and Rongdo literally translates to 'the lower part of a valley.'

The walk started off fairly steep and difficult, but after a few short breaks, we made it to the top. One of the villagers began to show us the sacred sites in the mountains while we were resting on top. He pointed out various naturally formed shapes like the chos se puti (volumes of Buddhist text), the chodme rangbar (self-formed lamp), and some rock-shaped animals that are associated with Mahakala (Gonbo).

We could clearly see what the two villagers were explaining from a distance, including how the flame of the lamp was burning and how the dog appeared to be almost leaping over a mountain. My brother-in-law was prostrating himself before each and every sacred location that the villagers had pointed out, but when I tried to zoom in to them with my camera, all I could see were some rock formations. I was thinking about how, as a result of technology and scientific knowledge, many people's faith is gradually eroding, particularly among the youth. The decline in pilgrimage is a blatant indication that today's generation does not see the mountains and valleys as sacred. Meanwhile, we kept walking into the valley. The two guides had been describing and pointing out the sacred spots continuously. Bodhisattvas—self-formed protectors—and scenes from the famous *Epic of King Gesar* are all present in the mountains on both sides of the valley. The villagers knew exactly where they were, but it was difficult for us to discern each and every feature accurately. By this time, I had given up using my camera's zoom to focus on specific areas.

We arrived at a place called Hipti at around half past eight, where we observed a massive sacred juniper tree and the ruined meditation home of a hermit by the name of Tsampa Nurboo. We took a little break there and shared some snacks and drinks. My brother-in-law joined the two villagers as they began to sing a traditional song. After three hours of walking, we came across some shade from a tree, some quick snacks and drinks, and listening to a wonderful folk song that almost put me to sleep. Suddenly, one of the villagers said, 'Dr sahib, let's go. We need to get to the Gonpa before the Loskyong (lamp that burns for a year) is lit.'

At around half past nine, we arrived at the Gonpa (temple), located at the base of the mountain on which the Mahakala is naturally formed. The villagers there gave us a warm welcome and offered us tea, cookies and local bread (Khambir).

While the locals were busy preparing lunch for the pilgrims and themselves, the monk was praying inside the temple. We went inside the temple, did chanting and prostration, offered a Khatag (a traditional scarf) to the altar, and then left. When I came out of the temple, I kept looking at the route in case any other pilgrims followed us; but to my surprise, no one was to be seen. We were informed that a resident of the Rongdo village, who was married in Deskit, another village, was this year's sponsor of the Loskyong, a lamp that shines for a year. The lamp should have been lit by now. The sponsor, the villagers and the monk were all close to the lamp. Following some chanting by the monk, the sponsor lit the candle, and everyone prayed and wished for Mahakala's blessing.

We made our way farther into the valley to the sacred waterfall, known as Nagaraksha or Lhui Gonbo, guided by a few villagers. From Gonpa, the journey took around an hour. When we got there, we witnessed the waterfall gushing forth from a height with a lot of force. Behind the waterfall, we saw a black rock with the figure of Nagaraksha. We were told that sinners should stay away from the waterfall because, as they get closer, the water drenches them. The protector also turns down their offerings. On the other hand, good people are able to see a rainbow on the water, and their offerings settle beneath the water. When we arrived at the waterfall, my brother-in-law had the incense and smoke offerings ready. After we prayed and prostrated, we were astonished to see a rainbow rise over the waterfall. Our offerings were accepted, we felt incredibly blessed and delighted.

After spending about an hour there, we made our way back to the Gonpa, stopping along the way to see the fields and little homes where the villagers of Rongdo reside with their animals during the summer season. I continued to think about the cause of the fall of the pilgrims as I made my way down.

I questioned a villager about his thoughts on the decline in pilgrims. 'People may visit in large numbers in the years to come,' he replied, 'but my concern is that people's faith in the sacred landscapes is dwindling. If people don't have faith, it's simply like coming for an excursion or a picnic. There are many sacred lakes in Ladakh, and when our elders go on pilgrimage, they used to see Buddhist monuments and religious sites in the lake. But today, no one sees them because people don't have faith.'

I was thinking about how my brother-in-law and I were different at this point. At practically every holy place, he was worshipping and prostrating, but I wasn't. I was aware that my faith was not as strong as his, but I still had an immense amount of respect for the faith and belief in sacred landscapes that my forefathers had.

When we returned to the Gonpa, the monk was still chanting, and a few villagers were also worshipping inside the temple. We took a break in the courtyard, where the villagers were offering us tea and lunch, because we were becoming a little tired by this point. After a while, the monk joined us, and we had a wonderful talk about the decline in pilgrimage as well as the decline in public faith. I explained to them that in a culture like Ladakh's, which is closely related to the landscape in which it survives, the connections between sacred space and other aspects of the region's culture are essential to our understanding of the region's heritage. That's why it is crucial to preserve these traditions for future generations. The issue is not unique to Rongdo Gonbo; a similar situation exists everywhere in Ladakh.

The knowledge of these sacred sites is fast disappearing as many rituals associated with them are no longer practised, and the younger generation has little knowledge of their significance. I told them, while appreciating the village communities, that for generations, the villages have conserved these locations, and that even now the village community still plays a significant role in maintaining their sacredness. 'Respect for sacred landscapes is still evident in Ladakh, and it is hoped that this will continue in the future,' the monk went on, echoing what I had told the locals. We thanked the residents and the monk and went back to the village.

Even though I haven't been to Rongdo Gonbo in a while, I've heard that the number of pilgrims has increased in recent years. Here, I recall the words of one of the villagers, who stated that while many people may visit, a decline in faith is worrying. My only wish is that visitors come with faith and devotion rather than for picnics and excursions that can compromise the sacredness of the valley.

A Day | A Home | Stok

Manasi Chokshi

The seventeen-kilometre ride from Leh to Stok takes you through a variety of landscapes: tall, wooded forests, brown snow-capped mountains, extensive barren lands, bridges over the gushing Sindhu river, and quiet villages dotted with cemeteries, chortens, prayer wheels, anganwadis, primary health care centres and old and new houses. The ride takes you on a variety of roads, heavy traffic to driving in absolute isolation; each turn brings a pleasant surprise.

Situated at an elevation, the winding roads in Stok are a combination of uphill and downhill, with quiet houses shaded by trees and guarded by compound walls. A typical Ladakhi house is difficult to spot nowadays. It is built in stone or brick, with plastered walls, roofs made in poplar, wooden beams and willow twigs covered with straw, grass, mud and clay; sometimes even with the dung of cows, donkeys or horses to increase its solidness. The exterior is simple with windows being the only decorative elements. These have a double lintel that is carved and recessed. This type of façade is also seen on government buildings, hospitals, hotels, etc., in Leh. For a Ladakhi, the summer months of June to September are extremely crucial. Owing to extreme winters, the people here

Credits: Subin Selva

prepare early for surviving the harsh months of November to March. The duties of agriculture, rearing animals, home repairs and maintenance, drying and stacking food grains and vegetables, etc., keep them completely on their toes. And thus, the Ladakhis have a summer house or a yarsa. A yarsa is built near the fields to ease the constant effort required during summer.

Spotting one such yarsa, its entrance is a metal gate that opens into a backyard of towering and gently swaying poplar trees. Under the shade of these is a pathway that leads you to a large field that is the front yard of the house. The house belongs to a family of three: Angchok, a sepoy in the Indian Army currently posted in Lucknow; his wife, a homemaker, Tacring Lamo; and his daughter Padma, a student of Masters in Rural Studies at the University of Jammu. 'I joined the army as a sipahi for financial stability,' says Angchok, the owner of the eighty-year-old house. 'I have taken a few days off so I can be home with family and help with the summer chores like cultivation, harvest, storage, repair, maintenance of the house, etc.'

The narrow pathway takes you via the field to a staircase that takes you to the first level of the house (the lower level is reserved for the cattle), which opens into a long passage with rooms on both sides. The living room is a large formal sitting space with a traditional bukhari in the centre. Right above the bukhari is a puncture in the roof for smoke from the traditional fireplace. Below the puncture is a big, beautiful but worn-out hand-crocheted rug. The southern wall of the room is lined with a series of timber and glass-paned windows. Below the window is a long low seat cushioned and insulated with thick woollen mats. At the southern corner of the living room is a big traditional metal stove with wooden shelves, with neatly stacked pots and pans above it. 'Nowadays, the metal stove is kept like an artefact, used for cooking feasts and special family meals, and we also have another kitchen across the living room,' says Angchok, welcoming us to his home and showing us around. The kitchen across the room is a typical urban kitchen with a working L-shaped platform, storage cabinets, cooking gadgets and a sink. The kitchen also has windows like in the living room, with linear seating insulated with thick woollen mats. The rooms are supported with thick and heavy timber beams and timber columns with decorative capitals, or the kazhu. The floors above the beams are spanned by thin and uniform poplar rafters. The family uses the wood from the trees in their backyard to repair or replace any of these rafters. In the gaps and slits between the beam and columns are old family photographs, religious garlands, etc.

'These mats are made by me,' says Lamo, Angchok's wife, a thin lady in her mid-forties. 'I weave, knit, crochet and I also stitch. These mats, that rug, are all made by me. What to do in the winter months? He is on duty; one should be active. The summer months are different, extremely busy. We plough, sow, grow, harvest and store grains, like wheat and barley, vegetables like turnips, carrots, potatoes, cauliflowers, peas, etc., for the winter. A pit is made on earth and all the fresh produce is stored in it.' Dressed in a salwar kameez with a sweater, Lamo is a homemaker leading an almost traditional lifestyle.

She enthusiastically demonstrates the use of the big metal stove in the room. 'See, we insert logs of wood and cow dung, from this side of the stove. On top, we keep the vessels to cook in. And from the opposite side, the ash is removed. This one is made of metal and is very old. I love saving up old knick-knacks. I will show you'. She empties a small pouch on the small centre table and shows her collection of old objects. An old multi-use pen knife, some ornamental keys, jewellery, beads, buttons, etc. In the living room also stands a small refrigerator along which is kept a tall, tubular, quiver shaped object. She says, 'This one is something I am very fond of. I can show you how we make the tea. Let me make some butter tea for you. You must try it.' With that she begins making the butter tea or gur gur chai in the tube-shaped tea maker.

The gur gur chai is made using yak butter, salt, soda, milk and tea leaves called Zarcha. Demonstrating, Lamo adds all the ingredients in the gur gur carefully and churns it for a few minutes. Adding boiling water to this concoction, she then filters and transfers the pale pink brew into a thermal flask. Lamo serves the tea with a dollop of butter, in ceramic cups, with a side of a big thaltek. A thaltek is a savoury bread made of barley. It is perfectly round, thick and dense. Sitting cross-legged under the line of windows, accompanied by conversations with the family, the brew is hydrating and refreshing. Lamo also demonstrates the best way to eat the thaltek—chunks dunked in the gur gur chai.

'Today, only three of us live here,' says Angchok. 'We used to be a joint family. During winters, in this very room, we would light up a bukhari, and all ten or twelve of us would be sitting around it till late at night. You must visit in the winters to witness the festivals and culture here; especially our new year, Losar. Losar is the Ladakhi new year, a five-day long affair, with religious rituals in the house and the local monasteries along with social meets and greets. We light diyas, make and offer sweet bread to the gods and relatives, decorate our homes, streets, temples and monasteries. A lot of weddings also happen during the winters. Weddings are usually a one-day ritual, but they have other rituals on the preceding days.'

Credits: Subin Selva

Credits: Subin Selva

Padma, Angchok's daughter, home for the summer break, chimes in: 'In Ladakh, women are given a lot of liberty for education, career choices, even in finding suitors. In fact, pursuing a master's and doctorate are very common amongst the women here. The girls are studying more and more. In contrast, the boys are discontinuing their education and becoming financially independent. They find lucrative job and entrepreneur opportunities, like being taxi drivers, trekking managers, tour guides, guesthouse owners, biking guides, bike rental providers, etc. There is a great disconnect and so it gets difficult to find appropriate matches.'

Further adding to the conversation, Angchok's cousin sister, Yangchun, says, 'I have pursued a bachelor's in arts. I live with my father, two brothers, sisters-in-law, and nephews and nieces. My mother passed away last month after a long illness and since then I have been taking care of the house. My brothers work in Leh City and my sisters-in-law work in schools. We have two houses, an old one that is under repairs, which is like this house, and another one right next to it, recently built. I can take you there.'

The conversations flow comfortably: the ecology of the region, the water consumption of tourists, the late summers and harsh winters, the politics of the country, development in Ladakh, the room rentals, travel, and so on. After taking some pictures of the beautiful house, the fields, the knick-knacks, some shots with the family and hungrily gulping the tea and bread, we bid our goodbye to Angchok and visit Yangchun's home, just a few houses away.

Yangchun's house looks like an imitation of the mud and wood house, with a much more contemporary, neater and finished appearance. Roofed with a layer of insulated material and aluminium, the house has a formal entrance porch, with a passage at the end of which is the kitchen. The living room has 'c' shaped seating of regular sofa height, with windows above it. The seating has a couple of the Ladakhi centre tables with carvings on it. The fourth side of the room has all their kitchenware neatly stacked and on display in glass cabinets. In the corner also sits a big LED TV, and in the centre of the ceiling a hole for the vent of the bukhari. The kitchen has a standing platform, a chimney and all the modern cooking gadgets.

A wooden staircase leads you to the upper floor that has two bedrooms and a big temple room, with the shrine of Buddha and the goddess Tara. It has a beautifully painted ornamental entrance way, cabinets and other furniture painted in the Thangka style. The house has a 'solarium' or a 'sunroom' that faces the south to maximally absorb the sun's heat in the winters. The house is fully carpeted, relying only on the bukhari. The house is however devoid of adjoining fields, and they largely rely on the city for their supplies.

The experience of the ride, the hearty encounter with Angchok and his family, and the warm conversations left behind a hearty, earthy and satiating aftertaste, just like the gur gur chai and thaltek! A sense of rootedness and pride in Ladakhi culture, combined with an ambition to rise as a community, is evident here, and this attitude is remarkable. This rootedness, pride and ambition, along with a keen eye on the modern systems of education, marriage, politics, ecology, technology, etc., is perhaps the way forward for the people and region of Ladakh. The terrain may be hard, the climate unforgiving and the villages remote; the people, however, are civilised, self-sustaining and happy.

Story of Many Lands: Nubra

Saylee Soundalgekar

The merchandise that passes from Yarkund, via Ladakh to
Hindustan consists of gold, ducats from Russia, in old coins
from Bokhara, and a small quantity also finds its way from
Bultistan; silver, silks, and porcelain from China; musks, furs …

… From Hindustan to Yarkund are carried madder, pearls,
English calicoes, Dacca muslins, chintzes, kimbals, or golden
cloth of Benares, shields, indigos, henna, spices, sugar, tabashir …
—Andrew Harvey, *A Journey in Ladakh: Encounters with Buddhism* (1983)

This story is about a fertile oasis in the cold desert, a potluck of
cultures, the trade hub of the Silk Route. Nubra, a town in the
newly formed Union Territory of Ladakh, is a legitimate goldmine.
The Gazetteer of India (1854) reads: 'Gold has been found in the
sands of the river Shy Yok, but its collection is discouraged by
the authorities, apparently for combined motives of policy and
superstition.'

Nubra lies in northern Ladakh and can be accessed by one of the
highest motorable roads in the world. The mighty Khardungla
pass, at 18,380 feet, dictates accessibility to this town from Leh,

Credits: Author

Credits: Riddhima Khedkar

with its military-controlled checkpoints of North and South Pullu. With a gradual drop in altitude from North Pullu, Nubra is covered with farmlands, vegetable gardens, clear waters, and is enveloped by towering Karakoram–Himalaya peaks.

Wangyal sat there by the River Shy Yok, building a zen stone sculpture and meditating. Owner of a reputed homestay in the Nubra Valley, Wangyal has inherited the land, camels and riches of his forefathers, who were then the traders of kaleen (carpets). 'Integrating China silk, Indian weaves, Persian calligraphy and abstracts,' he tells us, 'the carpets are the finest blend of cultures and an apt remnant of the Silk Route.'

Wangyal owns two Bactrian camels. The double-humped camels are a gift to Ladakh from the Central Asian countries. They were first introduced in Kashmir by Hazrat Mir Sayeed Ali Hamdani, a revered Sufi saint. When he, along with 700 companions, travelled to Kashmir for the first time in AD 872. The caravan used these camels to cross the cold desert from Iran via the Silk Route that stretched from Sian in China to Antioch in Syria. Subsequent trips in AD 874 and AD 876 were also made on these animals.

In the decades to come, as the trade came to a halt, the traders abandoned the camels. They were then rendered useless to the Ladakhi soil and rare species of Bactrian camels turned out to be a burden to families who adopted them. 'They were difficult to maintain. The families then were unaware of the animal diet and we had trouble growing our food, let alone the camel! There was a time when the camel count had reduced to forty in the complete region. In the past few decades, times have changed. With easy access, awareness, literacy, trade and tourism have been a blessing to us. There are over 430 camels in Ladakh now. Purchase cost for a camel is around Rs. 80,000, and each year, the season yields us an output of 3 to 5 lakhs.' Nubra and surrounding areas now produce and export buckthorn—fodder for the cold desert. With high fertility, Nubra is home to alfalfa grass and elm from the Middle East, potatoes from the Dutch missionaries, opium from the British and berries from Kashmir. 'We used to be self-sufficient; each home had a seed bank with the exotics and native apricots and barley,' says Wangyal as he pulls out a Yarkant bread. 'Now these are experience centres for tourists.'

Nubra was a 'low-lying' land en route from Hoshiarpur in Punjab to Yarkant in present-day China. 'It was the easiest of all mountainous routes,' he says as he recalls the oral histories from his ancestors. 'You will find Nubra homes loaded with Yarkandi Pulav, Yarkandi bread and Chhurpe (dried yak cheese).' Charasa Fort in Nubra still hosts the royal family with inherited delicacies, utensils from across the Silk Route and Chaang (local alcohol). 'We owe our life to the land, its diversity, and the wealth it has brought us.' Nubra once had direct links with Afghanistan, China, the Middle East, Iraq, Tibet and Europe. Today, geographical boundaries have stopped trade.

'Our lifestyle has changed a lot over the years. Local food and occupations are dominated by the takeaway economy. Our shops sell packaged water and processed food. ATVs over sand dunes have rendered the bumps flat.'

Nubra is one of the top trending tourist destinations in the country, home to sites filled with 'Instagram-able' locations that offer a sense of accomplishment, organic food that is rarely available anywhere in India and ample no-network zones. With people flocking the second highest motorable point of Khardungla, the infinite riverbanks with pristine waters and the dunes amidst the cold desert, Wangyal questioned the past that flew by.

'But then comes the winter,' he says. 'The land is frozen, and the Khardungla is closed. Nubra wakes up to a shared warmth. It gives us more time with family and friends. Though freezing cold, our social life is the most exclusive and fulfilling now.'

Credits: Nilza Wangmo Lonpo (Owner, Alchi Kitchen)

Culinary Couture

Ruma Pratihar

Ladakh's most influential couturist found herself in a conundrum just a year after she established Namza Dining in Leh. Padma Yangchan, with a successful fashion label, Namza, that she co-founded in 2016 with Jigmet Diskit, was persuaded by friends to start a little cafe at the lovely garden adjoining the land on which her store stood. She began the namesake cafe and accrued profits in its first year itself, when it was booked to full capacity on most days. 'I made it "reservations-only" for some respite, but this only increased the demand,' she laughs. She was overwhelmed, not owing to the cafe's growing popularity, however, but because she was dissatisfied. 'I added the regular fare to my menu that made tourists happy in Ladakh. Momos, tandoori, pizza and pasta. The format worked, even though I had no background in food or hospitality. But I was not happy.'

Because, you see, Padma has a penchant for excellence and her work has always been rooted in authenticity. The term Namza translates to clothing in Ladakhi language, and the name had lent itself to the cafe. The label had successfully revived Ladakh's cultural identity through couture, putting to use its heritage weaving and dyeing techniques. She had employed women from remote parts of Ladakh, converting their everyday skill of weaving utilitarian daily-use clothes to high fashion that graced the London Fashion Week in 2019. Nothing about Padma's vision was ordinary, and that extended to the cafe as well.

'You see, I am not Punjabi or Italian. I cannot make the best tandooris nor pizza,' she states matter-of-factly. 'I thought why not do the same with food also. When I started, none of the food was documented. People knew little beyond momos, thupka, sku and chutagi.'

She looks pensively into the distance and continues, 'Some places served paba and gyathuk, but it never tasted how it did when I was growing up.' The food that she mentions as a crucial part of her childhood is from the time she spent holidaying with her grandparents in Nurla, a village in eastern Ladakh. 'Food at my parents' house consisted of dal, chawal and sabzi. But in the village, I ate traditional food. Only apricot or walnut oil was used in the cooking.' She recalls drapu: 'It is a soupy pasta. It involves making a paste of apricot kernels and walnut, which is tempered, followed by adding wheat. It is a heat-inducing food and is eaten in winter.'

Padma's favourite, however, is the gyuma, a sausage, made with minced mutton mixed with fat and rice, stuffed inside intestines and cooked. It's also on the menu of Namza Dining, and to me it is quite the hero. It is presented with a portion of local bread and two chutneys, red and green. The gyuma, bread and chutney could be eaten together or individually, each a different experience from the other. The sausage, with every bite, coats your tongue with fatty goodness, making you salivate as the minced mutton and rice mixture offers texture, flavour and comfort. A familiar palate, only elevated. The chutney is sharp, hot and garlicky enough to cut through the richness and clean your palate for the next bite. It is a welcome cycle of eating and repeating. Much of the menu at Namza Dining now is shaped by Padma's vacations back in the village. These memories are also layered with her late grandfather's food stories. 'He was an Indian prisoner of war in China. They were apparently served beef every day. He spoke about times when he also got the meat of wild ass. I would get extremely excited, trying to mentally conjure the textures and flavours,' she laughs.

Although she has an appetite for adventure, she can't stomach the idea of blood and visiting the abattoir. 'There were things I liked but couldn't get myself to cook. There's this other gyuma, which is made of blood, barley and cumin. Another preparation involved mixing milk with some herbs and spices, which is poured into goat lungs that are sealed and cooked. It is sliced and served. I do it for special customers on request, but the blood sausage is something I cannot do since it involves going to slaughterhouses and collecting blood.'

While these memories are still fresh and served as the starting point for her culinary adventure, it was quite the challenge to forge Ladakh's culinary identity. 'I don't remember any elaborate meals. Even during Losar, our new year, momo and thupka were the main meals. On one of the Losar days, we make food for the dead and offer it to them at the graveyard. The leftovers are shared by the neighbours. But again, it wasn't anything exotic, paba and maybe some boiled mutton.'

But whatever she made in the present day never tasted the same. 'It was not even close to what I ate in my village. Once my father mentioned how all the food that we ate back in the day was brought by the mountains, it had no pesticides or medicine.

And then it struck me that we should start foraging.' Although foraging is now the buzzword in modern cooking, it is extremely difficult and painstaking given the climate and terrain. 'Ladakh is huge and we have only six months of season time to research; the roads and passes are blocked from November till May,' says the lady who shuttles her time between Delhi and Leh, looking after her space in the national capital.

It has taken her seven years to document everything that she brings to the table, literally. 'In May, we get capers shoots, nettles and wild chives. July is the time for wild cumin and many vegetables.' There are also influences from other regions since Leh was once a trading town on the Silk Route linking Tibet, Kashmir, Central Asia and Yarkand. 'Some food like buckwheat and drapu travelled from Skardu and the Hunza Valley; one of our kind married a lady from Baltistan, and she got Balti cuisine,' she says, citing her eventual mastery of the Yarkandi Pulao as a major milestone in her journey.

'There was a legend about Yarkhandi traders that their pulao was so rich, ghee would drip from the elbows of those who ate it. My neighbours in Leh were originally from Yarkhand and my mother was always excited to visit them on Eid since they made the best pulao. It was apparently cooked for hours. One day, I asked my neighbour for a recipe. He told me the crux of the preparation and I began experimenting. One day, my mother declared I had achieved the exact taste!'

With innumerable accolades, Namza Dining has taken quite the pride of place in Ladakh's culinary landscape. But Padma also has those days when the odd tourist walks in expecting tandooris and makhnis laden with tadka. 'If you come in here expecting cliches or richly spiced heavy food, then that's silly, in fact almost disrespectful. Please don't ask me for achaar and raita with Yarkandi Pulao. However, there was also one person who ate the food and his feedback was, "your best thing is the saunf", and we both laughed! And that's fine by me.' Today, Namza Dining also has its own little vegetable garden, which also grows chamomile. Seven years and counting, from generating profits in its first year to redefining Ladakhi cuisine, the journey has just begun.

Dr Azad with Jackie (1999)

Saving Jackie

Shashi Velath

Amid thundering artillery and flashing explosions, one thought consumed Dr Azad Ahmad Ahanger. 'What can I do to keep them safe?' In the biting cold of Dras, a place where stark mountains reached up to touch the sky, a chilling wind blew through Kargil in the summer of 1999. With courage in his heart, he hatched an audacious plan. He would move all the animals under his care to a safe shelter. As he moved through the rugged terrain, each step was a delicate dance of trust between man and animal. With his gentle yet firm touch, he guided Jackie over steep paths and narrow ledges.

Several months before the outbreak of the Kargil War, the Jammu and Kashmir Animal Husbandry Department imported a Haflinger horse from Austria. This horse was both huge and bulky. The goal was to cross-breed the Austrian Haflinger with local mares, in the hope that their progeny would be better, heftier and more productive for the local population.

While tending to the unique yak and cow cross-breeds of the region, such as the Dzo and Tul, Dr Azad became particularly attached to the horse he named Jackie. With gentle eyes and a sleek golden mane, Jackie stood out among the rough-hewn, mountain-adapted animals of Dras. Dr Azad travelled from village to village, asking the locals about the health of their livestock, and marvelled at the resilience and adaptability of the local animals.

In the winter of 1998, months before the Kargil War broke out, the temperatures plummeted to unimaginable lows. The doctor's bond with Jackie only deepened. They would wander together through the snowy landscape, Jackie's hooves crunching on the frozen ground. Dr Azad used to freely visit the army canteen. He would meet his friends in the army to go on a walk every evening, from Dras to a place they called 'the beach', a sandy stretch that resembled a real beach, where the river water would flow forcefully, spreading like waves. They would sit there, chatting and enjoying the scenery. During the weekends he would join the locals to play cricket.

But one summer morning, he received news that the army had restricted movements of the locals, and the civilians were not allowed to visit the army canteen. He was told that something had happened atop the mountains, and the army suspected there might have been some infiltration. He noticed the serene calmness of Dras gave way to frenetic military activities, and his friends were not available for evening walks. Then, one day, all of a sudden, he spotted helicopters breaking through the clouds and bombarding the mountain tops. War had broken out. The next morning, around 10.30, he discovered that his staff had begun to leave. By evening, almost all his staff had abandoned the clinic, and the entire village had emptied out.

Dr Azad was gripped with anxiety. 'What do I do now with these animals? I can't leave them!' His clinic—or rather, his small veterinary hospital—was more than just a place for treating animals. He had established a small dairy farm to sustain the staff. Whatever extra milk the farm could produce, it would be sold to the local people, generating some revenue. It was a simple operation, but it was meaningful.

The next day, Dr Azad noticed his last remaining staff member, Razak, quietly packing up to leave. He approached him, concerned. 'Razak, where are you going? The animals need to be fed. Where are you going?' Razak's response was sharp and filled with fear. 'Sir, I cannot stay here. No, Sir. I have a family. I don't want to get killed here. I'm leaving.'

Dr Azad was left alone with his animals, including Jackie, a feeling of desperation in his chest. 'How will I take care of them?' he wondered, increasingly anxious. 'How will I make arrangements for their fodder, their upkeep?' The empty clinic felt more and more desolate.

On the third morning of the Kargil War, the warm-hearted veterinarian's hopes were shattered when a shell struck his office. The entire room was destroyed. Thankfully, his living quarters were located a slight distance from the office, sparing them from the destruction. That night, he was jolted awake at regular intervals by blast after blast, but he remained indoors, not daring to venture out.

As he lay there, a realisation hit him: continuing to feed the animals under these circumstances would be unsustainable. As the war intensified, the doctor faced a critical decision that would test the very core of his beliefs. Jackie, along with other animals, were at risk as the fighting closed in on their location. To save them would mean putting his own life in grave danger. He urgently called senior officials in the animal husbandry department in Kargil and explained the dire situation, emphasising that his office had been hit and safety was now a serious concern. They promptly directed him to move the animals to a sheltered place known as Khandiyal, around ten kilometres from Dras.

Dr Azad managed to secure a truck from Kargil, ready to transport the dairy animals, which included two cows, a bull and a calf. But the journey's preparation came to a sudden halt when he faced an unexpected obstacle: Jackie just refused to climb onto the truck. Dr Azad's mind raced as he tried every trick in the book, gentle persuasion, firm commands. He cajoled and coaxed, his voice softening to a plea and then hardening to a demand. But Jackie remained unmoved, his hooves planted firmly on the ground, his eyes wide but unyielding.

But Jackie eventually gave in.

As the days turned into weeks, the situation stabilised slightly. Navigating the dangerous terrain to feed and care for the animals became a daily routine. Dr Azad found solace in the presence of the animals under his care, comforted by their trusting eyes. The war ended, but the memories lingered. Years later, Dr Azad still thinks back to those times, to the lines by Gautam Buddha that inspired him—'Unseen they suffer, unheard they cry. In agony, they linger; in silence, they die.' For the doctor it's a reminder, a lesson that compassion and kindness must always guide us, even in the most challenging times.

As the war wound down, the echoes of battle fading into a mournful silence, he found himself sitting with Jackie one day, looking over the quieter fields of Dras. The landscape was still bare, scarred by the ferocity of a conflict that had torn through their lives. But amidst the destruction, there was a calmness settling in, a sense of coming to terms with what had happened, a tranquillity born from survival and resilience.

'Jackie,' he whispered, his voice barely more than a breath, the weight of emotions making it hard to speak. His ears flicked towards Dr Azad, and they looked at each other with deep understanding. 'We made it.'

The author of this account, a seasoned journalist with extensive experience covering war and conflict, had the opportunity to meet Dr Azad in Dras while reporting on the Kargil War.

An eco-resort in Ladakh carrying out organic farming

Disposing Waste, the Ladakhi Way

Shobhan Sachan

Chhuk-po nor-ri mi-gang, gya-tso chhu-yi mi-gang
(Wealth does not satisfy a rich person; water does not satisfy the sea)
Chhu-zyig be-na gyal, mi-zyig dum-na gyal
(Diverted water is safe, [and] people living together are safe)
Phu-a kang-ri chags-na, do-a gyam-tso khi
(When glacier forms in Phu (high altitude areas), the ocean is formed in the lower parts)
—Angchok et al., (2008)

'It's all related!' says Lamo, a middle-aged, free-spirited, cheerful woman. She was a barista, and a caretaker of the public convenience facility at Pagir Cafe. As the locals and tourists flocked to the cafe, Lamo scurried around the place picking up glasses, leftover food, tissue papers and food cartons from the tables. I sat there, working on my laptop, waiting for Lamo to finish her duties. At noon, she sat beside me and said, 'Sorry to keep you waiting. The season is just getting started. It will be the same for the next two months.' While volunteering in Ladakh for three months, I had the opportunity to meet Lamo and immerse myself in the enchanting landscapes and vibrant culture of Ladakh last spring. I was first introduced to the Ladakhi way of waste management while I spent my days working at a local NGO that was working to promote sustainable development.

'How is it all related?' I asked Lamo, continuing from the conversation we were having earlier in the morning. 'Remember the poem I recited for you? It was about how water is supposed to be treated,' Lamo explained. 'It is something that we Ladakhis learn as children. We elect our "Chhurpon"—Lord of Water. He is responsible for water management. We also sign a Kamgya—a contract between the Chhurpon and the community members. But recently, ever since tourism started giving the state easy money, I've felt the culture disappearing.'

Lamo was silent. She looked out at the busy market street. She could see bottled water. 'We are in a cold and dry state. We conserve water. We maintain the Bandabas or Bandobasti for water management. Its list contains the groups of farmers residing in a particular village. It's a contract that tells us how much water to consume—farming, drinking, our animals and so on.'

'What about waste management then?' I asked.

Lamo chuckled. 'We never had a concept called "waste". Remember: it's all related. Each product has its purpose. This is a traditional technological system and ancient practice to keep our surroundings clean and in harmony with nature.'

True to their heritage, Ladakhis have long viewed waste not as a burden, but as a resource that can be repurposed to serve in challenging weather conditions. Initiated in 1974, tourism in Leh district is today almost fifty years old. During this period, approximately 2,700,000 tourists have visited Leh district (population in 1971 around 53,000 and estimated 147,000 in 2021) of which around 900,000 are foreigners and 1,800,000 are Indians.[1] Ladakh, which never needed a dumping site, now has one in the Bombgarh area, approximately a kilometre or so from Leh City. The construction of the Leh road in 1966 and the construction of an airport in 1985 marked a turning point in Ladakh's development. This accessibility resulted in an increase of tourists from 500 in the 1990s to 2,05,000 in 2017.[2] There were only twenty-four hotels in all of Ladakh in the 1980s. In the last four decades, the number of hotels increased to 670, with 60 per cent located in the city of Leh.[3] The influx of tourists and foreign influence altered the once-balanced ecosystem, bringing new waste management problems.

'What about human and domestic waste then?' I asked Lamo.

'We believe in designing our homes cosmologically. The topmost floor is given to the heavenly world. We have a prayer room and gathering rooms there. The floors below are for the human world. We have habitable places, bedrooms, a fireplace and dry toilets there. The ground floor is for stable storage and, to answer you, for human domestic waste management.

'Before you ask what dry toilets are: standing in front of the Mahabodhi International Meditation Centre, Leh, you can see a poster that reads, "Traditional Ladakhi toilets do not waste or pollute water like water toilets, and they also produce useful manure for fields and trees. Please throw a shovelful of earth down

---

1 Pelliciardi, V. . (2021). Factors Affecting International and National Tourist Arrivals (1974-2020) in Leh District (U.T. Ladakh, India). European Journal of Sustainable Development, 10(1), 736. https://doi.org/10.14207/ejsd.2021.v10n1p736
2 Kumar, S. (2019). A self-governance approach to solving the water crisis in Ladakh, India: Ice Stupa Project. University of Twente. http://purl.utwente.nl/essays/79522
3 Khandekar, N. (2017). Ladakh responds to tourism's demands on its water. The Third Pole. https://www.thethirdpole.net/2017/07/26/ladakh-water-tourism-demands-india/ [Accessed 18 May 2024].

the hole after each use." These dry toilets are essentially both water-saving and useful in the winters. That's the answer to your question about dry toilets. We have a dry toilet built on the first floor with a hole in the slab. After using the toilet, a mixture of ash and mud was shovelled into the hole. The room below acted as a collection or decomposition room. It did not have any openings, and access to this room was from the exterior of the house. The absence of ventilation helped the decomposition of human excreta. Once or twice a year each home produces manure for the fields as well, and water is not wasted! But now modern homes have taps and flushes, putting pressure on the water requirements of locals and tourists. Manure is not produced anymore.'

As my volunteering experience unfolded, I had the privilege of witnessing Ladakh's timeless wisdom in action. The region's sustainability practices were evident in every aspect of life. Ladakhis showcased their resourcefulness and their commitment to minimising wastage in everything, from communal gatherings to vibrant festivals. One captivating example was the Ladakhi Goncha, the traditional attire donned by locals. I observed how each Goncha had a cleverly designed pocket and a tie-up string to carry a reusable tumbler, a simple yet ingenious way to reduce the need for disposable cutlery during communal events. This tradition spoke volumes about the Ladakhis' respect for resources and embodied the spirit of togetherness that defined their way of life.

As my three months in Ladakh came to a close, I found myself deeply moved by the Ladakhis' profound belief in karma, which instilled in them a strong sense of responsibility towards their natural surroundings. The region's scenic landscapes, often compared to the moon, were not immune to the consequences of irresponsible tourism. Still, the Ladakhis remain resolute in their commitment to preserving their heritage. In my moments of reflection, I realised that Ladakh's waste management journey was a microcosm of the global environmental crisis.

The frequent floods due to over-melting glaciers in the terrain regions and pressure on resources due to increasing tourist activities adequately demonstrate the impact of global warming. It underscores the need for a collective effort to embrace sustainable practices and cherish the delicate balance between humans and nature.

As I bade farewell to Ladakh, I carried within me the memories of its breathtaking beauty and the wisdom of its people. With her unwavering dedication at the Pagir Cafe, Lamo had been more than a source of information; she had become a beacon of inspiration, embodying the Ladakhis' indomitable spirit and legacy of sustainable living.

AIR T

Thukje Ley: Living Music Museum

Vaishnavi Subramanya

If you hop on the Leh–Srinagar highway from Phey and walk a couple of kilometres towards the Indus, following a few hand-painted signboards, you'll find yourself at the SECMOL (Students' Educational and Cultural Movement of Ladakh). That might be the easiest—and perhaps the only—way to get there. The school, started by Sonam Wangchuk, is well known for a lot of things. But one name brings a smile across everyone's face: Thukje ley. 'I hear someone's here to meet me. But why me?' she exclaims as she comes out of her dorm.

Thukje ley has been blind from birth. She grew up listening to her father sing folk songs. After a few serendipitous encounters, she found herself following in his footsteps. Even though she is cut off from most of the world, she longs for simpler times. 'Gone are the days when phones weren't a thing, when television wasn't a thing, when even vehicles were a rare occurrence. In those days, people had the patience to sit and listen.'

Thukje always wanted to become a teacher. 'I have two brothers in the police force but I hate it. I love non-violent professions like teaching and medicine.' But she immediately adds, 'Too much peace isn't good, either. Then, the students don't learn to be confident in life.' The clock strikes one, and as the dining hall gets flooded with students, they chorus a Zhung Lu (traditional Ladakhi song) before starting lunch. Upon requesting another recitation, she shrugs. 'Oh, songs are too long. I'll tell you a story instead.'

The folktale she recites to us is about a magpie who seeks food and shelter in the winter from three sisters. The sisters all have different responses and, in the end, get served justly for their generosity. While being a typical moral folktale, the story speaks of the winters in Ladakh. The land being high and arid, people survived on herding and subsistence agriculture until it recently took to tourism.

But, as the tourists disappear and the temperatures drop below zero, Ladakhis reunite with their families and spend the rest of the winters resting, playing ice hockey and celebrating festivals of Losar and Mamami. Dried fruits and vegetables, from throughout the year, are stored in bunkers to be used for these times. Ice from the lakes has to be broken to procure water. The story also speaks of the magpies that are only found in the summers, and how despite being as common as the crows for the rest of the country, are said to bring good luck if they nest in one's home.

Thukje ley started her journey in 2002, with the Education Awareness and Women's Alliance campaigns, and she travelled across the country. 'The first month at SECMOL was awful for me. I didn't know the way to walk or talk, unlike my home. With practice, things got vastly better—and look, I'm still here!' She feels, though, that for a person who has friends all across the country, her Hindi is very weak. '*Ladakhi toh sab bolte hai, na!* (Everyone speaks Ladakhi, right!) she says in perfect Hindi. 'Songs

are meant to be sung. If you don't practise every day, you lose them.'
The mode of music consumption plays a pivotal role in its longevity.

The 1980s saw a massive increase in the production of Zhung Lus
by All India Radio and Doordarshan Television. With the advent
of tourism, there was a balancing act to embrace other cultures
while preserving their own. In this context, the engagement of the
youth with Ladakhi songs was mostly through radio or television.
In the more remote villages, it is still through festivities, communal
performances and completions that also involve traditional
instruments. Monks of the village specialise in these instruments.
They are called to play certain types of music for different events
like festivals, horse racing, historical plays, etc. While Zhung Lus are
about Buddhist histories and philosophies, Yul Lus (Ladakhi village
songs) talk of everyday rituals and trivial things. It is popularly joked
that there are Ladakhi songs about everything.

Thukje ley is a treasure chest of Zhung Lus and Yul Lus. At the age
of fifty, she recalls 170 of them, to be precise. There is no recorded
history for many of them for, until about forty years ago, Ladakhi
was not commonly written, but a spoken vernacular. So, for most
of our lifetimes, Thukje ley remains our living museum.

Khapulu Fort

Credits: Author

Balti: An Account of Twin Districts

Dr Ghulam Mehdi

Many tribal people in modern India are located in remote and inhospitable terrains and are nonetheless devoted to their traditional ways of life. The Balti community is one such tribe that is unique from other ethnic groups in terms of art, custom, culture, literature, language, dress, food habits and so on. The Balti tribe historically, geographically and ethnically belongs to Baltistan, under unlawful occupation by Pakistan since 1947. The Baltis have been influenced by many religious systems, ethno-linguistic groups and rulers throughout history, resulting in modifications in their art, culture, language and other parts of life.

During the Indo–Pak War of 1947–48, the erstwhile state of Jammu and Kashmir was partitioned, resulting in the split of Baltis across the Line of Control. Because of this partition, the majority of Baltis have remained in Baltistan, with just a few villages remaining in Ladakh; during the Indo–Pak War of 1971, a few more villages were captured from Pakistan's illegal occupation. In the recent time, Balti cultural and linguistic specialists have been aware of the truth and begun to negotiate their sociocultural and linguistic identity in light of the growing processes of inter-sociocultural connections with the other tribes in Leh and Kargil.

As a result, the purpose of the paper by Dr Mehdi is to investigate socio-cultural and linguistic accounts of the Balti tribe of Ladakh.[1]

The Baltis of Ladakh are one of the many such communities who have shifted from traditional pastoral life to sedentary agriculture and horticulture. Historically, however, the community has witnessed major waves of change ranging from Bonism to Buddhism, then Islamisation and Nationalisation, since the tenth century, and it is said that the Islamic practice in these communities is unique and quite different from Muslim societies in the rest of India.

A sociological insight on the acculturation process sheds light on the question of how synthesis of culture due to cultural contacts shaped the present culture of the Balti community. It is true that the mountainous communities have been following a distinct societal structure, such as marriage, family and the kinship system. Habitat formation and their sustenance have been ecologically sensitive as their myths, folktales and folk songs depict the environment in which they live.

There have been three major developments among the Baltis. For starters, greater tourism has resulted in increased engagement with the outside world. Second, the Ladakh Autonomous Hill Development Council (Kargil and Leh) and the Union Territory of Ladakh are engaged in development activities. Third, agriculture and horticulture are undergoing a technological revolution. Anthropologists, in particular, have attempted to explain the process of development in culture through acculturation, when culture traits discovered or invented at one place reach at another place; such a process is called 'diffusion'. However, when the whole

---

1 Kumar, S. (2019). A self-governance approach to solving the water crisis in Ladakh, India: Ice Stupa Project. University of Twente. http://purl.utwente.nl/essays/79522

system of life in a culture begins to change under the influence of any other culture, it is called the process of acculturation. The trinity of the habitat, economy and society, and its functional or dialectical relationships, are explored in a holistic manner to ascertain the nature and extent of change (transition) in the Balti community.

The presence of the Baltis poses three questions: how have isolated geography, topography, climate conditions shaped the cultural history of Baltis in the district of Leh? What factors and forces led the community to transform its past nomadic life to sedentarization and settlement? And what external factors influence the habitat and socio-economic activities of Baltis as part of the modernisation process?

***

Balti is the language spoken by the Balti people of Baltistan and Ladakh. The language used here differs from Standard Tibetan. Many of the Old Tibetan sounds that were lost in Standard Tibetan may still be found in Balti. Furthermore, only polysyllabic words have a basic pitch accent system; Standard Tibetan has a complex and separate pitch system based on syllable outlines.

Balti is widely spoken in Pakistan's Gilgit–Baltistan region of Skardu, Sigar, Glutari, Ganchey, Rangdu, Khaplu and Karmang. Balti is also spoken in Karachi, Lahore, Peshawar, Islamabad, Quetta and other cities in Pakistan. They are the major speakers in Changmar, Bogdang, Chulunkha, Gharari, Turtuk, Tyakshi, and Thang in Leh district, as well as Hardas, Karkichu, Lato, and Balti Bazaar in Kargil district; after partitioned, immigrants from Baltistan, Kargil, and Turtuk spoke it in Dehradun, Nainital,

Ambadi, Shimla, Vikasnagar, and other North Indian cities. In Balti, there are four variants or dialects.[2] Urdu vocabulary has been incorporated into local dialects and languages, notably Balti, since Pakistan took control of the region in 1948 and recaptured a few villages from the Indian Army in the year 1971. Balti now lacks local names and terminology for dozens of newly developed and introduced items. It rather uses Urdu, Ladakh, Purki and English terms. Many honorifics from Tibetan dialects and other languages have been retained by Balti.[3]

Speaking of Baltis in Kargil, they are predominantly found in three villages in Kargil district—Hardas, Lato and Karkichu—situated on the left bank of the Dras river, a couple of miles from the main Kargil town, are predominantly Balti.[4] In Leh—in a bold attempt to defend Siachen and Ladakh—the Indian Army, led by the renowned Colonel Chewang Rinchin, captured 804 square kilometres of land during the 1971 conflict, along with the Thang, Tyakshi, Turtuk, Gharari and Chulunkha. However, Bogdang and Changmar were already under Indian administration before 1971.[5]

The significance of the proposed study lies in the context of the transformation that has engulfed a community, which is giving up its primordial base and customary institutions and practices and getting more integrated in mainstream society (Purki and Lasdakhi) and more familiar with its normative values and ideology. The study pertinently deals with the following questions: what is happening to communities like the Baltis of Leh and Kargil district?

---

2 Balti Language Encyclopaedia, Science News & Research Reviews, Academic accelerator.
3 Kazmi, Abbas 1984 "The Balti Lok Geet" Published by National Institute of Folk Heritage, Islamabad.
4 Gupta, Radhika (2014) "Poetics and Politics of Borderland Dwelling: Baltis in Kargil", ideas of south asia.
5 An online article "Turtuk - The Crown Jewel of Baltistan", published by, www.shadowsgalore.com

Are they losing their customary practices, their culture, language, customs and traditions and getting closer to the other groups, or trying to maintain and restore their own culture in a modified way? The answers to these questions suggest a trend and direction that will be of great importance to their future. The pressure of traditional forces, as also the relative isolation of the community, has retained them in traditional socio-cultural settings. Apart from the influence of Ladakhi culture, the communities keep on perpetuating certain specific cultural traits.

Story derived from a research paper by Dr Mehdi (Mehdi, Dr G., "Balti Language and Dialect: An Ethnographic Account of Ladakh's Twin Districts", Ladakh).

A Ladakhi kitchen in Kargil

From Stok village, Gyab Thago museum

A Ladakhi Kitchen

Rashida Kousar (Kalikhan)

In days of yore, the chansa's hearth,
Where Ladakh's soul found mirth and warmth.
There meals were shared and prayers were said,
And guests with open arms were led.
Here, laughter echoed, chang was poured,
In this beloved place adored.
Such is our tradition's grace,
What beauty in this sacred space.

Andrew Harvey, in the book *A Journey in Ladakh* (1983), writes about a song that was sung by a monk as they gathered for the sunset. He says that the Ladakhi culture rejoices in the feeling of happiness in everyday life. That there are no unhappy love songs in traditional folk literature. And that real wisdom is joy. The kitchen is a place to be joyful, to relish the joy of food, of nutrition, of what Mother Nature gives us.

We, the people of Ladakh, live a simple life in harsh weather. We have a simple existence. The traditional homes were built partly with stone and partly with the sun-dried mud brick, and the

Ladakhi kitchen is mystical. It tells the stories of generations, of seasons that went by, of the produce that trade and land brought, and of evolving cultures. It is the most important space at home. The design of the house revolves with the kitchen as the focal point. It serves as the home's gathering place. Families gather in this room to sleep, pray, cook and eat meals around the thab (fireplace).

'Who needs multiple rooms in chilly winters with separate heating devices, when we can all cuddle up in the core!' says my grandpa. Back in 1884, the King of Jammu, Maharaja Pratap Singh, gave the Moravian missionaries permission to live and work in the region. One important piece of equipment they brought along with them was the huge cast-iron stove with an inbuilt baking portion. 'It was from this that the Indian Army and Ladakhi home developed the metal thab,' says grandpa.

My grandpa, Haji Abdul Majeed (Kalikhan), now ninety-six years old, is a worshipper of the valley. A man of the Indian Army, he recalls the struggle for food, for a job, and the challenge of running a family in the 1950s in this cold desert. 'As a child, the kitchen was an invisible cave,' he says, his eyes shining with glee. 'It was dimly lit, as the room was full of smoke and the roof and wall were embodied with soot. The flicker of the hearth was the only source of light and heat. Mother used to go to the market, sometimes to the forest to get wood and cow dung for the hearth.

'Back then the biggest weakness of the hearth was the absence of a proper piped outlet. A metal pipe was too expensive to be purchased for a single household. The soot present in the room was normally inhaled by the family, and it was normal for our eyes to burn. The heat from the fire was so essential that unfortunately the health problems had to be ignored.' Sitting on the porch, looking at his old motorbike, grandpa runs down memory lane. 'The houses had a flat roof built with poplar wood (dungma) and willow wood (taloo). Above the poplar and willow layer, people placed a dried thatch. The roof was then finished with mud mortar.' Grandpa paused as I handed him the butter tea. 'Skid–duk,' he continued. 'Happy–sad. We believe the wood is supposed to be placed in odd numbers. The roof should end with wood laid in odd numbers for happiness.'

Ladakhi homes range from one to three storeys. The doors and windows are small in order to minimise the entry of cold waves and keep the house warm. The kitchen has three essential components: thab (hearth), langs (shelves) and tal (seating).

The most important part of the kitchen is the clay oven, or the hearth, what we call the thab. It needs skilled labour to give it a good shape and design. The thab is attached to shelves (langs) and the thamba (special seating placed for a woman in charge of cooking and lighting the fire). In the morning, the mother (thabgyalmo: queen of the house) comes and prays to the thab. Only after that does the mother start cooking.

Food is prepared on the thab, and the family gathers around it to eat and talk. The thab used to be a clay hearth, and goatskin was used as bellows to accelerate the burning. It normally had three seats so that cooking could be done in three pots. In this, firewood, cow dung, horse dung and dry organic waste were used as fuel. While serving the food to guests, the mother of the house says a proverb: *Gesmo metnang, gesmo dzat ta don* (Even if it's not great food, make the best of it and eat it with pleasure).

Doltok

Gormo

Tibril Mislang

Thab at Lonpo House, Leh

Credits: Author

A kitchen window in Turtuk Village

Credits: Author

A modern kitchen - Stok village (gyab thago)

The thab has three main symbolic signs on it, namely: Nubru, Palfi and Padma. It is the most beautiful and attractive part of the kitchen. It is always made up of wood, and traditionally, its designs are very simple. Most of the utensils are displayed here. It gives a rich look to houses. There are traditional utensils placed here—like the tibril, mislang, thagu, doltok, gormo, sangthal and every essential utensil used while cooking. There is another very simple type of shelf called taksha, made inside walls with wooden planks or else built of wood.

The seating line along the wall is called tal. There are certain seating rules. You sit in order of age—from elder to younger—and the mother of the house serves food in front of the tal. This table is small and simple, whereas more recent tables are larger in size and richly carved and painted. This tal is divided into two, namely tralgo and traljuk. Tralgo means higher table, where more important guests sit, and traljuk means the end of the sitting line, where people with lower social status sit. This system isn't used as often today, though. 'The old practices have led to stereotypical thinking among the elder generation,' says grandpa. 'The old days were harsh because of the climate, low accessibility and poorer connectivity. The missionaries, the Buddhists and trade have been a blessing in disguise.' He continues to treasure the joyful moments when he and his fellow Buddhists and other friends share festivities and food, and of course celebrate together.

The Childhood of Anay Putith

Sonam Dechen

Today is Anay Putith's turn (Chures) to water her fields under the scorching sun. With wet shoes and socks, she is busy with her duties. Anay's little nephew runs into the room to watch his favourite cartoon show.

'I remember how happy we were when our turn came to water the fields,' she says. 'The refreshing dive in the pond, smearing our bodies with mud, getting sunburned, and playing with friends while our parents were busy.' The baby at the corner of the veranda cries with her face down, and Anay knows it's time for a diaper change. She shouts to the elder one to bring a diaper, but he ignores her a few times. When Anay shouts furiously and repeatedly to her nephew, he comes out with a diaper and quickly goes back to watch the cartoon.

Anay whispers to herself, 'During our time, we didn't have diapers but were brought up in a Tsalu' (a sag filled with powder of goat and ibex droppings). She remembers going to collect ibex droppings from the mountains when she was young. A warm stone (Tsando) is kept in the Tsalu which keeps the Tsalu warm and makes it comfortable for the baby. Anay said that Tsalu is not only to keep the baby warm and dry but also has many positive effects for the baby's health even when s/he grows up.

She had seen her younger brother being brought up that way. She also recalls her mother singing lullabies. Anay remembers that she also used to sing lullabies to her brother. She smiles and says, 'Sometimes, I slept while singing lullabies to my brother. Now, every aspect of social and family life has changed. Today's children have not seen Tsalu and they don't listen to lullabies from their elders. Today, a lullaby on Alexa can do the job.' In the name of modernisation, according to her, people are forgetting the ancient wisdom of family bonding.

The little niece runs to get her teddy bear after the diaper change, excited to show me her new toys. When I ask about the toys available during her childhood, Anay replies, 'I don't remember even having a single toy at my time. The lid of a bottle, a chipped cup, and the lid of a jar were the best toys we used to own. We used to live with nature, and whatever was in nature was our toy.'

When asked about her favourite game when she was young, she said, Tulo (playing with five stones—the size of a marble), and Ale Rumbu, also known as Rumbu Thobcha (game played with small shells). While recalling how Rumbu is played, she said, 'We used to say, "*har har tug tug ama cho cho dang ta ama cho cho nyomste, tat tat pa tat jo pari gang na har young shig*".' Her friends, playing as the opponent, at the top of their voices, used to say, '*tug tug*'.

As we're engrossed in conversation, her nephew makes an unexpected appearance, coinciding with a sudden power outage. I turn towards him and ask, 'What's your favourite game?' Without hesitation: 'Candy Crush!'

Holding her nephew's hands, Anay worriedly says, 'Nowadays children are addicted to mobile phones, and they are confined to rooms that are not good for their health, especially their eyes and minds.' They have distanced themselves from Mother Nature, she says. I tell Anay that when we were at school, we used to play a game of student–teacher by using a few stones as students, with me and other students behaving as teachers. I vividly remember the students punishing some stones as if they were real misbehaving students.

The conversation doesn't end, but my sister calls us for lunch. As she prepares rice with vegetables, she uses mustard leaves, commonly known as Nagtigpa in my village. 'Nothing's better than a classic thukpa,' Anay says, eating a spoonful of rice. She tells us that her family, in earlier days, used to have their dinner under the moonlight.

She remembers her elder brother preparing dinner and her mom sitting in the corner and spinning wool to make sure that all children will have new traditional goncha dresses and pabu shoes made of wool with leather soles. At the same time, Anay complains that her grandson and granddaughter don't eat thukpa, making several excuses, including that it's too hot to have in the summer, the dough in the thukpa sticks to her mouth, and many other such excuses.

I ask about Anay's favourite festivals during her childhood. 'Losar and Nagrang (monastic festival of Matho Gonpa),' she says, after thinking for a while. 'During those festivals, I found it difficult to sleep at night. I was so excited. Especially thinking about the delicious foods during Losar and the mesmerising mask dances performed by the monks during the Nagrang festival.

'When we were children,' she goes on, 'during Losar, we were always so happy to witness the rituals being performed by the elders, delicious foods being served. My friends and I used to wait for the morning of the third day of Losar. On the third day, we go to collect ibex (skin) made of dough by the families during Losar. We would shout with happiness, "*Skin jik salang, skin jik salang, skin jik salang nati ama'i ma ne sui salchen.*" Sometimes, the families ran out of skin so we gave them a khura (a local snack), but they shattered their faces with sadness, got disheartened and refused to take it.

'In the evening, they would count ibexes and see who got the most. These ibexes were tied to a thread, and we played with them for several days until their heads and legs were broken and they were finally fed to the cows. These days, kids are unaware of these traditions. Now people hardly make ibexes during Losar.'

Anay Putith says that they used to prepare a special feast where elders made dinner for children. During the day, they would go to collect meat, flour, butter and mustard oil from the families. While asking for it, they would sing–

'*Hali ong phot na jho gang sala zad*
(Hali Ong… If you wish, give us a full coin)
Hali ong maphod na jho phad sala zad
(Hali Ong…If you don't wish, give us half a coin)
Hali ong chanda yospa bo sera gang
(Hali Ong…right pocket is full of gold)
Hali ong chanda younma bo rmul la gang
(Hali Ong… left pocket is full of silver)
Hali ong naja thugu tsangkala cha chamar jik salang lay. Lahore ra tabak skangs ta khong, cha cha la gu skyor ta khong, marnag po khil

basa khong markar ska gong basa.
(Hali Ong... give us tea leaves and butter. Please give us a plate
(from Lahore) full of meat (leg piece), mustard oil and butter)
Sta stara gangshig
(May the stable be filled with horses)
Ba bara gangshig
(May the cowshed be filled with cows)
Ralug ge lukra gangshig
(May the sheep pen be filled with goats and sheep)
Bru'i bang gna gangshig
(May the store be filled with grains).

This is a song sung by children during Losar when they would
gather at a place and celebrate by preparing meals. The song
started with a praise of the mother and father of the family. They
would, then, ask for ingredients to prepare their dinner. They
would, also, wish well for the family. Then the family would give
them the things they asked for.

'We were so happy with the things,' says Anay, 'and we didn't have
a music system, but we sang folk songs, had no fast food, and
had our feast as king and queen.' Similarly, during Nagrang, they
were excited because they got new dresses, and they didn't get
money as kids nowadays get. Nowadays, kids are given a pretty
good amount of money. They are not satisfied with a few bucks.

Anay never went to school, but her duty was to look after the
sheep and goats. 'Things have changed culturally and traditionally,
which has both good and bad impacts on our lives. I am worried
about the future generations, thinking about what will happen to them.'

Dras: Threads of Survival

Shashi Velath

In the shadow of the forbidding peaks, where the wind carries a chill that seems to cut through the soul, lies Dras, known as 'The Gateway to Ladakh'. Nestled within the Himalayas, it's a place where temperatures plummet to minus 20 or even minus 25, where the sun hides behind thick veils of clouds, and where frost paints a shimmering layer over everything. Here resides a community whose lives are bound to a terrain that is as barren as it is magnificent.

At my first glimpse of Dras, I found it more than a landscape; it was a painting of resilience, a narrative of survival and adaptation, told through layers of snow and rock. Through numerous visits, my eyes opened to a world where human ingenuity and natural rhythm were woven together in a delicate dance, where the army allows passing travellers to buy necessities from CSD (Canteen Stores Department) canteens, a gesture of cooperation and goodwill.

The people of Dras are bound to the land, and the land to them, in a symbiosis that speaks to the human spirit's capability to endure. Animal husbandry and livestock management are not merely part of the culture, but the very essence of life. It is in this mountain landscape, fit for animals but scarcely suitable for agriculture, that the people have found their unique way of coexisting with nature. The locals rear crosses of yak and cow, known as Dzo, Tul and Garr, with the suffix 'Mo' for females. These animals, with their short stature, better milk-yield than yaks, and robust nature, have adapted to the mountainous terrain. Their strange resistance against diseases is a testament to their wild nature. These animals are more than livestock. They're partners in survival: carrying loads, providing milk and offering warmth during the bitter winters.

The core of animal husbandry here lies in managing these animals, making them more productive and utilising their warmth during the frigid winters. Locals create sheds under their living rooms, with no ventilation, allowing the heat from the animals to warm their homes. In the summers, the animals are let loose, and the short-term agriculture of millet, jowar and other grasses, supplements the fodder imported from the Kashmir Valley. On every 21 December, they celebrate Losar Mela, a festival marking the beginning of Chillai Kalan, the harshest winter period in the valley. This forty-day period, beginning with the winter solstice, sees a drastic drop in temperatures. Every household slaughters an animal, mostly Dzomo or Tulmo, and hangs it in one of the rooms, preserving it for the brutal cold ahead.

The slaughter of a Dzomo is not mere ritual but a vital act of preparation for the brutal winter. The meat, left to freeze instantly in the biting cold, becomes a stockpile of sustenance. Throughout the winter, families cut pieces of this frozen treasure, cooking it as needed and relying on nature's preservation. This tradition has transcended survival tactics to become an integral element of their cultural identity and a symbol of their resilience.

But the tapestry of survival doesn't end with meat. During the summer months, families hoard turnips and potatoes, the products of a land that offers little but means everything to them. These vegetables, harvested with care, are stored for the winter in an age-old manner. The people dig deep pits, placing their hard-earned harvest inside and covering it with layers of grass and soil. Like a vault of hidden treasures, these pits keep the food fresh, waiting to be unearthed during the bleak winter months. When the time comes, the people of Dras dig up their hidden bounty and have a feast, a celebration of life and survival. It's a moment that encapsulates the spirit of Dras, where every act is a dance with nature, every tradition is a lesson in adaptation, and every meal is a testament to human ingenuity.

In this labyrinth of mountains, where the cold can be both a ruthless adversary and a preserving ally, the people of Dras have woven a way of life that is a beautiful blend of survival, culture and connection. Their practices are not mere solutions to problems; they are poetry written in the language of the land, a song sung in harmony with the winds of winter, and a dance choreographed to the rhythm of life. The people of Dras, primarily speakers of the Shina language, offer a fascinating insight into cultural connections. In Pakistan, Shina is the major language in Gilgit–Baltistan, spoken by over a million people, and a small community is also found in India, in the Gurez and Dras Valleys. The relationship with animals, especially donkeys, offer a profound insight into a society where animal husbandry is life itself.

In the rugged terrain of Dras, where human ingenuity meets nature's demands, donkeys play a surprising and vital role in the economic sustenance of the families. These humble creatures, often seen roaming the roads freely, aren't merely reared; they

Credits: Author

Credits: Author

serve as an unlikely bridge between the local community and the army posts atop the mountains.

In both winter and summer, the donkeys carry out a unique duty. The army, stationed at challenging heights, requires essential supplies like kerosene oil. The locals fulfil this need by placing canisters of oil on the backs of the donkeys and setting them on their way. The donkeys know their destination. They climb up to the post, deliver the canisters, and return, all without guidance.

There's a saying in Dras: 'If your son is not a gazetted officer, maintain a donkey; it will earn Rs 10,000 per month for you.' This simple yet profound practice is a window to the world of Dras, where every creature has a role, every action has a purpose, and where survival, culture and connection are woven in a remarkable tapestry of existence. It's a world where the wisdom of the land and the innovation of the people come together in a dance that sustains life in one of the most formidable terrains on earth. During my time in Dras, I learned about the extraordinary commitment required to navigate this rugged landscape. I was drawn into a world where every practice was a mark of resilience, every animal a part of existence, and every winter a triumph of life over the unyielding cold.

Dras is more than a location; it's a living, breathing entity. It's a world where simplicity meets complexity, where tradition meets innovation, and where every breath is a symbol of unyielding resilience. The people here seem untouched by the modern hustle and bustle. They are a people defined by innocence and warmth, living in a place where time seems to have stood still. The education level may be meagre in this remote region, but what the people lack in formal schooling, they more than make up for it in hospitality and human connection. To visit their homes is to experience the essence of their existence. They warmly welcome visitors into their modest homes, offering sincere gestures of hospitality. They offer butter, crafted from the milk of their beloved Dzomo accompanied by freshly made chapatis.

Communication here is a fascinating tapestry of languages. With outsiders, they converse in basic Urdu or Hindi, their words easily intelligible. Amongst themselves, they speak Shina, or as they refer to it, Drasi, a language that echoes their heritage and binds them to their land and to each other. Exploring the villages is a unique experience. Public transport can only take you so far in this rugged landscape. The houses, perched upon the hills, beckon you to walk, climb and immerse yourself in their world. The journey may be demanding, but it's a path that leads you to understand the true nature of Dras. The residents of Dras are accustomed to living in the second coldest place on earth. They start their day early and are seen tending to their livestock, which are crucial for their livelihood, or engaging in agriculture during the brief summer months. Their routing is simple.

In Dras, one finds not merely survival but a rich tapestry of existence, an ode to human adaptability, and the beauty of connection. It's a story of life's endless dance, its capacity to endure, adapt and flourish, even in the most formidable of terrains. It's a story that must be told, a heritage that must be preserved, and a lesson in humanity that must be shared.

Over Butter Chai

Manasi Chokshi

'Ladakh is a beautiful place,' says Shabir Mir, the owner of Pashmina Hut, a shop selling textiles and jewellery in the Leh main market. 'I have been to some very peaceful villages. These are extremely remote, where it can take you almost ten days to reach an urban area. *Itne dino mein, ek American tourist Leh–Ladakh mein trek karke, return flight leke apna office wapis join kar lega*' (An American tourist visiting Leh–Ladakh will complete a trek circuit and resume his routine life in these many days). And yet, people here are happy. Ladakhis are simple and straightforward. '*Ek dum sharif log hote hai ye. Apne kaam se kaam* (They have a lot of integrity. They focus on their work).'

Shabir, a Kashmiri, has been running the shop since 2010. Swiftly switching between English and Hindi, he is a man of multiple interests. A passionate mountaineer since childhood, Shabir would take tourist groups for treks around Ladakh, Himachal Pradesh and Kashmir. Preferring international tourists, he was registered as a trekking guide with tourist companies like Exodus in the UK, Snowline in the USA and Mountain Adventure in Denmark. 'The international tourists are conscious, self-reliant and, at times, self-trained for difficult terrains. In their hometowns, they even

Leh Market

Credits: Subin Selva

practise as per the conditions here. They are fun to trek with and lead very inspiring lives. Recently, Jonson Tours from Kashmir had assigned a Belgian lady, all of sixty-eight years! She trekked with me from Stok to Kangri and the Great Lakes of Ladakh. An absolutely fit and enthusiastic person. *Agar aapko interest hai, aap sab kar loge* (If you are keen, you can do anything). There are some difficult treks. The trek from Lamayuru to Wanla to Zanskar to Kibber, Lahaul and Spiti ending at Padum takes a fortnight to three weeks. The Chadar trek, which is enjoyed in winters, takes you through sub-zero temperatures. Both are risky expeditions, but people come. These treks are very fulfilling and take you to beautiful villages, mountain tops, forests, quaint barley fields, bliss and tranquillity.'

Today, a lot of these trails are becoming roads. Imagine this: you are trekking, and a car zooms past you. I am not sure why and for whom we are building these roads. It's not like these areas have a huge population. Where we need roads, there aren't any; where we don't need any, there are many! Some of the treks were most frequented by the Europeans, but sadly their popularity is on the decline because of these road interventions.

'*Lekin foreign tourist Ladakh main repeat hai, jaise Indian tourist Kashmir main. Aapko nikalne ka mann nahin karega Kashmir se* (Ladakh is a favourite destination with the international tourists, while Kashmir is more popular for Indian tourists. You would not want to leave Kashmir). Have you been to Kashmir? There are terrorists there,' he says with a smirk. Offering us two options of tea, Shabir bhai insists we try the namkeen chai.

'*Arey ye Kashmiri aur Ladakhi dono pite hai. Meethi wali har jagah mil jayegi. Aap try toh karo* (Oh, the pink tea is devoured by both

Kashmiris and Ladakhis. You will get the sweet and milky tea anywhere, but this one is a delicacy here. Try it)!' With sips of steaming chai, Shabir bhai continues talking about Kashmir. 'That is the image of Kashmir. That there are terrorists there, it is unsafe. Even we are fooled by the whole gung-ho of terrorism there. I have been settled here for thirty years now. Every year we see new types and levels of lies. A few years ago, I happened to read a headline in a popular newspaper regarding seven bomb blasts in Nishad Garden. My cousins own a photography stall in the vicinity. Worried, I called up to ask their whereabouts and learnt it was a big hoax. I was wondering how such a popular newspaper published such a story. It is a beautiful land that is torn apart for all these political reasons.

'Sab hai Kashmir main, siwai haalat ke. Kya aap books wagayra padhte ho? Mujhe bada interest hai history main. Toh aisa hai, that there are seven ways that connect us to Yarkand (today in China) (You get everything in Kashmir, other than your well-being. Do you read books? I have a huge interest in history. It's like this, that there are seven ways...).'

He continues, 'One of the silk routes goes via Kashmir, and Afghanistan further goes on to connect to Russia. Kashmir and Ladakh are some of the oldest international and intercontinental markets in the world. Their presence goes back to the early barter system days. Ladakh, situated amidst Pakistan, China and India, has very sensitive borders. And thus, these land connections are not in use today. Today, all routes are via air and sea, which are mostly longer ways to reach.

'Kashmir ka (Kashmir's) main client was Europe because of the Silk Route. The delicate weave and needle work in Pashmina that

is done in Kashmir is nowhere to be found in the world. It will easily cost you Rs 2,000 per square foot; 24,000 to 30,000 is what these shawls sell for. Then there is the carpet industry. An original silk carpet costs 6,500 per square foot, *aur humare yahan itna kharcha karne wala customer hi nai hai. Humare ilako mein itni thand hi nai hai* (And here, there's no customer who will spend this much. In our neighbourhoods, it's not even that cold).'

He goes on, 'The apple from Kashmir, the scientists and researchers say, is the best apple in the world. *Aap agar ek saal ke baad bhi bite loge, toh "crack!" karke aawaz aayegi* (If you eat it even after a whole year, you'll hear a "crack!" sound as you take a bite).' Walnuts, the giri variety, almonds and water chestnuts have the best harvest in the world. In the Hunza Valley, which lies today in Pakistan-occupied Kashmir, you have areas where there is a ban on plastic, chips and plastic bottled beverages. It is said to be one of the healthiest regions in the world, with the best apricot kernels!

'Seventy-five years after attaining freedom, I look forward to conserving cultural integrity, upholding lost traditions and opening up the uncharted paths of the Silk Route! 'Just imagine, if we open these land routes, imagine the rates of all the goods, imagine the pace at which it will reach our land. *Tees rupees main hum aap ko oil denge Mumbai mein. Humne plot toh khareed liya, lekin saare raste hi band kar diye* (We'll sell you oil for thirty rupees in Mumbai. We bought a plot of land, but they closed all the roads)!' he laughs heartily. From conversations that move from history to economics to arts to politics, Shabir goes on to explain how Kashmiri arts had such a long line of patronage and how today the Indian customer has no appreciation for it. He even mentions his attempt to start programmes with the Ladakhi shop-owners' association, that shall help the Indian customer and tourist understand the lineage of arts he belongs to. '*Yahan har type ka tourist ata hai. Lekin Indian wala bada hi ajeeb sa hai* (We get all kinds of tourists here. But the Indian is a strange one).' He adds, 'I feel the general Indian tourist needs orientation on high-altitude sickness. It is not the usual uneasiness. And the solution is not to sniff camphor. I find that the funniest. If camphor sniffing could substitute for oxygen, Neil Armstrong would have carried sacks of it on his space journey. When one goes to any new place, there are a couple of things the tourist can do to acclimatise—eat lots of freshly cut raw onions, have a rich breakfast that includes butter and other dairy fat, rest well, and apply Vaseline in the nostrils. You'll manage to breathe well with these little adaptations.'

Thinking of oddities like sniffing camphor, Shabir bhai also gets odd demands from tourists. 'Just a few days ago, a friend called from Delhi saying he wants to have the traditional Ladakhi chai in Leh. See, you will find very good Ladakhi culture and tradition in the remote villages. But in Leh, it is becoming more difficult day by day. Another friend from France wanted to see the snow leopard but in the mating season. Let me tell you something: Ladakh has some of the richest flora and fauna in the world. The snow leopard is a widely visible animal here; at least I have seen it several times.'

'I showed my French friend within five days of the trek, mating snow leopards and some families of the species as well. If you visit in July–August during the mountaineering season, I can take you to Ursi village, where deer cubs and cattle live together. The deer cubs wander inside the peoples' homes to simply lick the salty furniture surfaces. It is very cute to witness that. I won't have any photos to show you but I have a rule: I don't take pictures of myself at any peak or any sighting. I don't think it's a big deal, you see. Thanks to mountaineering, I started this business. The trekking companies I worked for would often ask me to take the tourists to stores selling art, shawls, jewellery and artefacts, where the companies also earned a commission on the sales. I saw the high profit margins these places had and thought I should set up a shop. I may not loot my customers, but *thoda bohot hum bhi kama lenge* (I may not loot my customers, but I'll earn a little bit here and there),' he said this with a lot of conviction.

Pashmina Hut is a shop with an average sized frontage, and has a range of clothes, shawls and jewellery. Once you walk into the shop, the humdrum of the market outside seems to disappear. It is quiet, with a burst of colours and reflective glass cabinets under the white glare of tube lights. The lower floor is dedicated to stone jewellery, racks of shawls, woollens, jackets, etc. The upper storey has apparels and ready-made woollen garments.

Shabir, through his experience, can immediately identify which customer is worth attending to, and which one is here for window shopping or 'time pass'. With one eye at the door of his shop, he continues the conversation with equal attention and ease.

'Corals and turquoise are traditional to Ladakhis. They wear this headgear called the Perakh, which is studded with blue turquoise, pearls and orange corals. It is expensive—easily worth lakhs, if made with the original turquoise and corals, and 25,000–30,000 if artificial ones. It balances very well with the dark tones of the goncha or sulmas that they wear. There are some other stones also that are native to Ladakh—aquamarine, amethyst, moonstone, sapphire-pink, blue and yellow. I also keep jewellery from other regions, Garnetts from Orissa, Jade from Ajmer, things like that.

'The Ladakhis wear their traditional attire for religious functions, weddings, prayer days, etc. Ladakhi women will also always own a coral and turquoise necklace embedded in 62.5 gm silver; four corals to either side of a big turquoise pendant. Their belts also have these stones studded in them. Typically, these heavy pieces are passed on as heirlooms to the eldest daughter. The property of the father is passed on to the eldest son. If the family has one more son, he will be sent to be a monk. If you want to witness more of Ladakhi culture, winters are the best time to be here.'

With this information, Shabir bhai goes on to narrate the story of Rinchin Shah, a fourteenth century Ladakhi king who ruled over the region. He was a Buddhist, dedicated to becoming a monk, but went on to become a popular sultan of Kashmir.

Being a true businessman, Shabir bhai further shows us various shawls and textiles. He proudly says how he can identify the origins of all the shawls simply based on the weaving style and the woollen texture. Textiles from Manali, Ladakh, Nepal and Tibet are very similar-looking, with thick threads, their T-borders and orthogonal motifs. The weave and wool both are thick and usually in dark colours. The Kashmiri shawls, on the other hand, have a finer weave, thinner woollen threads, lighter and pastel shades with floral motifs. However, a lot of these are also manufactured in Ludhiana and Amritsar as the authentic options are very thick and expensive for tourists in Leh.

From the long conversation with Shabir bhai, his varied interests in mountaineering, reading, precious stones and gems, textiles, culture, politics, speaks volumes of the person he is. His opinions, though very outright and controversial, come from critical observations and experiences. Though Shabir bhai is careful to not offend any Ladakhi sentiments, his yearning for Kashmir is hard to miss.

The regions of Tibet, Ladakh, Baltistan, Kashmir and Gilgit belonged to a larger holistic region that, once upon a time, thrived with exchanges of culture, trade and common histories. The restricted movement within these territories, due to political and military conflict, has led to an abrupt and awkward pause in activities that were once routine. This has brutally disrupted people's lives and displaced their sense of belonging, creating further undercurrents of animosity and rifts between communities. Today, these regions lie fragmented, all confused and struggling for their identities.

Of Places and Their Names

Dr Sonam Wangchuk

The original names of villages in Ladakh typically have historical, cultural, social or religious relevance. Village names are generally associated with features of landscapes, such as the lay of the land, water bodies, sacred groves, rock formations, fertility, as well as the biodiversity in or around the village. Over time, most village names have changed to varying extents, resulting in a loss of the original meaning of the name. In some cases, the change serves an easier pronunciation of a name. However, the worst corruption of place names has been perpetrated on highway milestones by the Border Road Organisation (BRO). The following are a selection of village names from the Nubra Valley, which have changed over time. The explanation for and interpretation of their original names are based on the oral histories collected from the area. There are possibly several other interpretations, which need to be researched and documented.

Sumoor: One story suggests that the village name is derived from 'Sum-yur', meaning 'three irrigation channels'. This is supported by the fact that the village is irrigated by three irrigation channels even today. Another belief is that the name of the village is derived from the words 'Sum Yul', meaning 'three settlements', as it is said that the villagers occupied two other places in the valley, before settling at the present site. The ruins of the old settlements are located in the upper reaches of the valley. Today, the name has been slightly changed to Sumoor or Sumur.

Tegar: The original name of the village is said to have been ldeb-dkar, meaning 'white plateau'. According to another interpretation, Nubra Valley resembles a sleeping demon. Since an mKhar (palace) was located just right of the demon's navel (ltea), the village was called lte-mkhar. Another belief is that on the hill above the village, there is a white line that runs across the middle of the hill, so it is called Sket kar (white belt). Later, it was named Kyagar, Tegar, and more recently Tiger. While most locals call it Kyagar, BRO's milestones proclaim that the village is called Tiger, which is also repeated in official survey maps. This is probably the most extreme change in the name of a village or locality in Nubra.

Murgi: The name is derived from the mountain above the village. 'Dngul' literally means 'silver' and 'ri' is 'mountain'. According to the book *Nubre Nas-shad* (*Nub-ra'i gnas-bshad*) by Urgyan Rigzin, the mountain has white lime (dkar-rtsi) and even some silver deposits at its core. Hence, the name of the village was Ngulri (dngul-ri) meaning 'silver mountain', which subsequently changed to Murgi.

Khardong: The name of the village was derived from an ancient palace (mKhar) and a fort (rDzong) situated at a place called Yuldoma, in the lower part of the village. The ruins of the fort are still visible. Later, the village name was changed to Khardong, which has been further changed by BRO and the Indian Army to Khardung on their milestones and souvenirs.

Pinchimik: The original name of this village was 'spang chhu-mig', meaning 'a spring emerging from a meadow'. According to oral sources, there was a beautiful meadow here where King Nyima Namgyal would come for picnics while residing at the Charasa Palace. The village is now known as Pinchimik.

Tertse/Terchey: The original name was said to be 'gter-sa', meaning 'treasure or store-place' (of sacred monuments). According to *Nubre Nas-shad* (*Nub-ra'i gnas-bshad*), there was a sacred Gomang stupa in the village, which contained sacred manuscripts and precious relics. The name has been slightly altered and is now commonly called Tertse or Terchey.

Khalsar: In the past, agricultural lands in the village were said to have been owned by a noble family from Nubra. As a result, the village was called Kharsa. Mkhar literally means 'palace' and 'sa' means land. The name has changed overtime and is now called Khalsar.

Kubet: There are two popular explanations for the name of the village. One, the village is situated at a place shaped like the Kumuda (water lily) flower. The second explanation claims that people would source stones for pottery from this place. The specific stone was called Kwat by the Balti potters, which is said to be mainly used in making stone pots (dolthog). Later, Kwat became Kubet.

Lakjung: The name of the village was 'legs-gzhung', literally meaning 'centre of prosperity'. It is said that the village was one of the earliest settlements in Nubra and was a prosperous village. The name has been slightly changed to Lakjung.

Khimi: The original name of the village is said to be 'skid-mi-gling', meaning 'village/place of happy people'. It's not clear how this name was changed to Khimi.

Skampuk: This village was originally called 'Gan-Phuk', meaning 'settlement of old people'. It is believed that an elderly couple first settled here, which gave the village its name. According to *Nub-ra'i gnas-bshad*, the area was very dry (sa-skam) and there was a sacred meditation cave (mtsams-phug) of Lama Samstan Chosphel near the village. It is believed that the village got its name through a combination of two words, skam and phug.

Chalungkha: The original name of the village was 'Chu-lung kha', which describes a place at the edge of a valley with water. 'Chhu-lung' means 'valley with water' and 'kha' means 'opening or front side'. Today, the village name has been slightly changed, and it is now known as Chalungkha.

Chamshen: The name of the village is derived from the self-emanated formation of Chamba Gonbo (Maitreya Buddha) in the upper reaches of the valley above the village. The original name is said to have been 'Cham-Chhen', meaning 'Great Maitreya' but this has now been changed to Chamshen.

Hunder: The village was originally known as 'sngon-dar', meaning 'the earliest growing (village)'. Hunder, Deskit and Lakjung are said to be the earliest settlements in Nubra. Today, the name has been changed to Hunder.

Charasa: The original name of this village was 'lchags-ra-sa', meaning 'an iron estate', as the mountain above the village has iron deposits. People from the village used to produce iron goods, including cooking utensils, such as iron stoves (lchags-thab), iron ladles (lchags-thum), trivets/tripods (lchags-sgyid) and tools for agricultural activities.

Digar: The original name of this village was 'bru'i-khal', meaning 'a load of grain', as the village produces an abundance of high-quality barley. Now the village has been named Digar or Digger.

Henachey: The original name of this village was 'dbyen-gnas chhe', meaning 'great solitary place'; it is now known as Henachey.

Udmaru: The name of the village is derived from the outline of the village, which looks like a flower: 'U-dum ba-ra', a fabulous and immensely large lotus in Tibetan literature.

While these names have undergone changes, there are several villages whose names remain true to their origins. This includes Tsati, Deskit, Rongdo, Taksha, Skuru, Kuri, etc. On the other hand, there are several village names like Tirit, Agyam, Panamik that are difficult to interpret. It is possible that these names have their origins in Hor-skat (Turki and other Central Asian dialects) as Nubra was located along the main routes that connected Ladakh and Central Asia. There are other villages such as Tyaksi, Bogdang and Turtuk, which I have not studied but hope to explore in the future.

The Oldest Willow Tree
and a Plateful of Memories

Ruma Pratihar

Sixty-five kilometres from Leh, and seventy-five from Stok, stands Ladakh's oldest willow tree in the monastic complex (also the oldest in Ladakh) at Alchi, a tiny parcel of land that is literally a breath of fresh air. It has almost all the virtues of Ladakh minus most of its adversities. The land is greener and its air is crisp, with the sun offering just the right amount of warmth filtered through massive green trees. The terrain is flatter, and definitely kinder. Alchi became popular on the tourist map because of Alchi's Kitchen, Nilza Wangmo's restaurant, which was featured in *Lonely Planet*, *The Wall Street Journal,* and, more recently, *Condé Nast Traveller* India. But this hamlet has also been home to the legend of Guru Rinchin Zangpo (AD 957–1055). It is said that Zangpo, credited with building 108 gompas across India and Tibet, rested in Alchi.

Before his onward journey, he stuck a willow stick into the earth, promising to construct a monastery if it flowered. It is said that the monastery was built in a night, alongside two more monasteries at Sumda and Mangyu, constructed the same night, with Zangpo present at all three locations. Today, alongside stories and serenity, Chef Wangmo evokes culinary memories from Stok on a plate at Alchi's Kitchen. Wangmo was raised in Stok Village, a stark contrast to Alchi, which is her paternal home. She lost her father before she was born and her mother returned to Stok, raising Wangmo in her hometown. 'I had my uncle and aunts, one of them was close to my age. I remember those days fondly; we had a lot of fun. Life was community-driven—farming, animal husbandry and such responsibilities were shared,' she reminisces.

But she is quick to break into a chuckle and mention, 'Although there was one thing that we were territorial about: our faeces! We used dry toilets and were jokingly told to not waste our "toilet" in other people's homes, to do it in our own houses!' And then of course, she mentions Losar, their new year. 'That's our main festival, celebrated across seven to nine days. Each village does it differently, but the spirit prevails with similar fervour.' And food is integral to the festival. 'On the nineth day, we make a special thupka called guthuk. 'Gu' translates to 'nine', and 'thuk' stands for 'thupka'. We make flour dough with chits in it. Each would mention one of the following: charcoal, salt, chilli, stone and so on. Depending on what chit you received, we'd determine each other's personalities.'

At the age of eight, she came to Leh to begin school. 'A little later than acceptable today,' she remarks, 'but back in the day we did not chase numbers and timelines.' However, for someone who learnt life lessons and the ways of mountain life early on, the conventional education system did not quite work. Wangmo struggled through her final years in school and had to drop out of higher studies owing to financial constraints. But she seems unfazed.

'I have no regrets because I learnt many life lessons and skills back in my village. From irrigation to cooking to identifying seeds, plants and herbs, my mother and grandmother have taught me a lot,' she asserts. And the rest she learnt from observation. She continues, 'I was fascinated watching my grandmother churn butter from buttermilk. When she made sku, she would press it with a certain technique to slightly caramelise it, that char; I still remember the taste.'

She eventually came to Alchi with her mother and grandfather to start life anew, at her father's ancestral property, of which she is the rightful heir. Initially, she had to fight the legal battle with her uncles, supported by her grandfather, but eventually her uncles decided to throw in the towel.

'Me and my grandfather decided to rent land. I got this piece of land, mostly barren, barring some apricot trees that are still there,' she says. The decision to turn to food, however, was a calling; a dream, literally, that she paid no heed to. 'I used to always dream of two things, and I would wake up petrified: gushing water, and a kitchen similar to this. I never thought or spoke about it to anyone.' With time, and after starting a homestay, she ventured into food. 'My husband and I came to this place and took the measurements, and when it all fell into place, I saw my dream materialise.'

Cut to the present day: she lives with her husband and a canine companion while her daughter studies in boarding school. There's a routine (and multiple accolades), and a life similar to her childhood in Stok. But with a slight difference. 'Alchi is slightly more traditional. For example, even while we follow the communal way of life with everyone contributing to agriculture, cultivation, etc., we have this custom, from May to August, from sowing to harvesting, women must wear the traditional attire. It is believed that not following this tradition may affect productivity.' But she immediately adds, 'There is no such practice for men.'

It's probably okay; throughout history women have shouldered a tad more responsibility than the other gender, as each of the sexes would like to believe about themselves. Alchi, otherwise, is a quaint, happy home to its 500 inhabitants. They cultivate their food, have no markets barring a few departmental stores and a little walkway dotted with shops selling souvenirs.

Whether by chance or plan, the location of Alchi's Kitchen could not have been better right at the bus stop, before the shops begin, leading you right to the gompa. With a belly full of food, you can choose to walk through the paved roads lined with souvenir stalls, or the backyards and untended lands adjacent to them. You may meander away into wilderness, underneath the shade of apricot trees, only for the prayer bells to trace your path towards the gompa.

Diary of a Road Trip

Saylee Soundalgekar

What did I know about Ladakh before I embarked on a journey through this newly formed state as a pillion passenger on a Royal Enfield Interceptor? Being in Ladakh altered all the preconceived notions I'd got from social media. With a canvas of clear blue skies, the painted mountains around me were truly a wonder. Ladakh has been known by several names throughout its history—Mang Yul Naris, owing to its Silk Route connections and the presence of many people; Kha-Chum-Pa, the land of snow; and Ma-La-Pho, as called by a Chinese traveller who visited the region in AD 400, referring to the 'red land'. Its present name, Ladakh, is derived from 'La-Tags', which in Tibetan means 'the land of high mountain passes'.

The geological history of Ladakh dates back to the time when the Tethys Sea and Gondwana land were unified masses of land and water. As the Indian subcontinent separated from the African landmass, it began its northward journey, ultimately colliding with other tectonic plates to form the Himalayan fold mountains. Interestingly, Ladakh's geology is even more complex, shaped by the movements of land masses and the emergence of mid-oceanic ridges, leading to the raising and subduction of land.

River Indus

Zoji La: A battlefield at -27 degrees, a path of blisters, here, the land elevates at 3,528 metres

Kargil: War fields spread over acres, the mountains roar 'victory'

Dah: One of the two Ladakhi villages of the Brokpa community, the people are believed to be descendents of the troops of Alexander the Great

Hambuting La and Indo-Aryan village: From Kargil to Leh, contrasting rugged landscapes and Batalik villages

First glimpse of the River Indus: A reflection of the purest white clouds, the river foam carves its way through the rocks, promising flourishing civilisations

Zanskar: Living examples of the rising and subductions of Earth's crust leading to the formation of land with a multicoloured, multilayered, raw and rugged terrain

Credits: Author

Zanskar and River Indus—the confluence: The Indus takes over to become one of the longest rivers in India

Credits: Author

Leh: The existence of a fertile valley and a town in all this wilderness of rock seems improbable

Credits: Author

South Pullu & Khardungla: The second highest motorable peak in the world, at 17,982 feet with an oxygen density of 49%

Credits: Author

North Pullu and Nubra: One path to the Karakoram range and the other to the Siachen glacier, lead to some of the most difficult terrains on earth

Mahe and Nyoma: The Ladakh Himalayan Ophiolites (LHO) are the remnants of the Tethys ocean and its mid-oceanic ridges

Hanle: Midnight beholds, the sight of a lifetime—The Milky Way galaxy

The region was once submerged beneath an ancient ocean, with fossils now being unearthed at heights of over 4,000 metres. The presence of palm fossils collected from Tsokar Lake suggests that palm trees once thrived in the region during the middle to late Eocene epoch, when Ladakh's elevation was lower than its present 5,000 metres. Today, Ladakh is situated in the Indus Suture Zone, dividing the Himalayas from the Karakoram range and the Tibetan plateau. Charcoal fossils further indicate early human habitation in this area.

From Kargil to Leh through Batalik village, steep climbs and smooth roads give a bird's eye view of the neighbouring settlements. One of the four last Indo-Aryan villages is tucked in these mountain slopes, camouflaged with green in summer and snow in winter. Ladakh has gold! But where exactly? Is there an active mine? Is it commercially extracted, or is it privately owned? Thornton's 1854 edition of *The Gazetteer of India* reveals that gold was indeed found in the sands of the Shyok river, but its collection was discouraged by authorities, perhaps due to a combination of policy and superstition. Some lamas predicted that harvesting the gold would lead to a failed harvest, and there was also a belief that the gold belonged to local deities who would inflict dreadful misfortunes on those who dared to seize it. The age-old anecdote held true; it has indeed 'protected' Ladakh's geological heritage.

PANGONG CLOTH HOUSE
KHANGSAR COMPLEX SHOP No-1. POLO GROUND ROAD NEW SHAR LEH

The Gonchas

Manasi Chokshi

The city of Leh is buzzing with tourist activity from June to September. Reaping economic benefits from operating cafes, artefact shops and such things during the short tourist season has encouraged a multitude of expats and immigrants from Nepal, Bihar and other neighbouring areas. So much so that it ends up masking the Ladakhi neighbourhoods and bazaars. Being the capital of Ladakh and a trading centre for centuries, bazaars trading in local wares prevail in the city. However, they appear to be deliberately staying away from prying tourists. Located in proximity of the popular tourist spots, these markets are flourishing but are veiled with chortens, stupas, sometimes parking lots, monasteries, bus stands and government buildings.

One such bazaar lies parallel to the popular Leh Market road. It is a mundane but typical world of Ladakhis shopping, exchanging pleasantries, women gossiping over a plate of momos, children playing, shopkeepers enjoying a hot cup of gur gur chai or simply busy in their shops. With most of the shops selling Western wear, footwear, woollen clothes, jackets, school uniforms, artefacts and jewellery, the Pangong Cloth Store is easily noticeable as one of the few shops dealing in traditional Ladakhi attire. Located near the

Gurudwara road, it is owned by an endearing Mr Dorje Namgyal, a medium built, short gentleman in his seventies with a receding hairline. Seated at the cash counter of the shop, Mr Namgyal, wearing a checked formal shirt, with a white half-sleeved sweater, and brown tinted glasses, says, 'We are fabric retailers and deal in custom-made Ladakhi traditional clothes. I was born and brought up near Pangong lake—that is why the name. I also own a shop across the street.' He points to Ladakhi Traditional Dress Shop Number 2. 'I have been running this business since the 1970s. Initially, my wife ran the store. Back then I had a full time government job at All India Radio as a clerk from 1974 to 2004. Since my retirement, my younger son and I run the shops.'

The Pangong Cloth Store is bright with freshly done interiors. Within the shop, there are tall, floor-to-ceiling shelves along the walls, stacked with rows of glimmering and textured fabric—some categorised by colour, some by the material type. Beautiful and bright coloured long robes in brocade, silk and satin are displayed on hangers at the entrance glass wall. There is also a line of dupattas, or long scarves with embellishments and golden tassels, on display. Inside the shop, there are a couple of mannequins clothed in long ankle length robes with a belt at the waist and a hat.

'We sell Ladakhi traditional clothes—*topi se leke juta tak* (hats to shoes.)' He goes on, 'A goncha is a full sleeved, ankle-length robe, worn by Ladakhi men and women both. The typical length for men is 52–53 inches, while for a lady it is 47–48 inches. The sleeves will be 22 inches, and the chest dimensions will differ. The difference between men's and women's goncha is that the one for women will have pleats at the waist. This is worn with a bead and coral-studded belt called the skerag.' He rattles off the technical details with consummate ease. 'A goncha resembles a long coat made of wool, velvet, cotton, polyester, or a combination of these, worn by men. The everyday goncha is usually black, grey, burgundy, or an earthen colour. The one worn during weddings and festive occasions is bright and made in imported brocade, silk or velvet. A sulma is a flowing robe worn by women. Unlike the goncha, a sulma is brightly coloured and is also made of wool, brocade, velvet or silk. It is stitched in such a way that it resembles an elegant ball gown. Plain or patterned, a sulma is symbolic for, and worn by, married women.'

Mr Namgyal further elaborates his business of textiles and customised gonchas. 'In this shop, we keep fabric suitable for bridal- and designer-wear. We have brocades and silks from Benares, suiting, woollen fabric and cotton from Amritsar and Surat.' He indicates various stacks of fabric placed on the shelves. Looking at the robed mannequins, he adds, 'I keep a few ready-made gonchas also. But my primary business is in making customised gonchas. That way, the shop becomes a one-stop destination for the customer. The customer shortlists and selects fabric of his or her choice. Then the design of the gonchas is suggested, either by the customer or by me when I give references from magazines or the internet. We even show some of our previous designs. Then measurements are taken, and the stitching is outsourced to tailors from neighbouring villages like Choglamsar, Moti market, etc.'

Saying so, he proceeds to show us the line of dupattas, or long scarves with embellishments and golden tassels. These are hung on a rod kept in a special artificially lit niche, near the glass wall. 'These dupattas are yogars. This is worn over the sulma. It is the showiest part of the bridal trousseau. We keep fabric for this as well.

'A yogar or lokpa are square capes draped by women around their shoulders to cover the back. These are made with sheepskin with the wool facing inside to keep the wearer warm. A yogar is embroidered using cotton or brocade silk, with rainbow tassels and sheep wool lining. A lokpa, on the other hand, is only made of sheepskin and is bereft of any design or embroidery.' The conversation is abruptly interrupted by a thin, old lady, whom he introduces as his neighbour. She walks in, plonks her shopping bags on the counter, drags a chair, sits and begins to talk with Mr Namgyal.

After the initial pleasantries, she joins in the conversation and says, 'Caps or topis are worn during important functions. Then there are traditional shoes also, or pabus. Pabus are pointed at the toe and made of Thikma—a tie and dye technique done in yellow, white and black colours on the maroon-coloured wool. The insole is made with jute and the outsole with yak or buffalo's skin. They keep the feet warm.'

After a few more updates from Mr Namgyal, she swiftly picks up her shopping bags and bids us goodbye. The Ladakhi couture is incomplete without mentioning the stone-studded amulet worn in the neck, the kau; the silver jewellery with corals, bead-studded headgear, or peraks; headgear with flowers, or tepi. Some of these are symbolic to the communities and regions the Ladakhi belongs to.

With one eye on the Pangong Cloth Store, Mr Namgyal leads us to the shop across the road that has an old, dusty look to it. Though not as fancy as the Pangong Cloth Store, the collection is equally diverse, with woollen gonchas, skerags, yogars, satins, cottons, lacey fabrics, ready-made gonchas, jackets and a couple of kurtas on display. Showing us the fabric on display, he says, 'This shop has similar things but at affordable rates, so everyone is empowered to buy traditional dresses. According to me, traditional clothes must be worn every day. The authorities have made it mandatory for all to wear the traditional clothes for all government functions and holidays! A new rule also says it must be worn once a week. The people of course continue to wear these for festivals, weddings and religious functions, hence there is a high demand for them.'

Being a popular national and international tourist destination, one does observe a shift in preference to modern day dressing like pants, shirts, T-shirts, denims, kurtas, salwar kameez, etc., amongst the locals. The small, local shops in this bazaar cater to these fashion trends, but not to the extent of having fast fashion brands and showrooms.

Designer brands like 'Jigmat Couture' and 'Namza Couture', which are culturally and socially conscious, are contemporising and reviving the regional indigenous styles and textiles. This continues to induce a sense of pride and awareness in the minds of people. Further, the gonchas, sulmas and the yogars, with their accessories, are convenient to wear and are able to combat the harsh climate of the region. With shops like that of Dorje Namgyal that cater to all types of people, these traditional clothes won't be vanishing anytime soon.[1]

---

1 Kaur, Manmeet. 'Traditional Costumes of Ladakh for Men and Women.' Leh–Ladakh India Blog, December 28, 2020. https://www.lehladakhindia.com/blog/traditional-dresses-of-ladakh/.

Confessions of a Serial Entrepreneur

Ruma Pratihar

Ladakh slows you down in more ways than one, and for good measure. Blanketed in snow for six months, followed by the 'season' as the locals and outsiders call it, the land breathes at its own rhythm, its heartbeat echoing through the mountains and valleys. Tsetan Dolma seems to have caught its pulse bang on—and she seems to be sprinting at the speed of light. She knows her land, its people and the mighty mountains. Today, she heads her travel company and also has a cafe in Leh under her wing. And she's an active part of the Ladakh Mountain Guides Association.

'I don't know what I am, there are too many things,' she says. But she knows what she's doing. More importantly, why she's doing it. Her high cheekbones and sharp nose are the exact shade of pink that indicates sunburn, a telltale sign of high-altitude treks. She says, 'I've chosen mountaineering as my career. I realised I wanted to be in tourism a long time ago.

'During my school vacations, I worked as a tourist porter on treks, carrying 18–25 kilos on my back. I did the Markha Valley and Sham Valley trek twice, or maybe thrice.' She would eventually go back to her village when school reopened, resuming the activity only after she finished high school. But not before a massive shift in her perspective and outlook on life.

'In 2009, I failed my tenth standard exams. I then went to the Students' Educational and Cultural Movement of Ladakh (SECMOL) where they encouraged application-based learning. They don't force reading or writing but imbibe leadership, spoken English and so on. There were instances when I struggled; some seniors gave me a tough time but I cleared all my papers in a year. And, more importantly, I understood the importance of education.'

Her nascent days, till she finished school, were mostly spent in the mountains as a child who was happiest with her goats in the hilly terrain. 'I grew up in a village near Khalsi with around thirty families. Every family would take turns taking our domesticated animals to the mountains. I would go on Sundays, and I was happiest with them, but after SECMOL and clearing my exams, I never went back to them.'

But, in a way, she did go back to them. She came to Leh to pursue her undergraduate studies in 2011. And the culture (read capital) shock was palpable. 'I didn't have the best financial condition, I used to get Rs 100 a month from my elder brother. Oil cost Rs 65 a litre. I spent some money on basic stationery and bought Parle-G biscuits with the rest.' But that's also when she was picked up by a travel agency as she knew the trekking routes and spoke English, all while pursuing distance education from Indira Gandhi National Open University.

She founded Ladakh Family Tour and Travel in 2016, which was soon succeeded by De Khambir, a cute eatery near Leh's main market. Dolma goes on to explain, 'During our expeditions, we stayed in homestays. You know, we stopped at Shushul near Thiksey on the way to Hemis, Lamayuru, when we were headed to Sham Valley. The tourists were keen on eating traditional, local food. That's when I decided to start De Khambir.'

Khambir is the name of the local Ladakhi bread. It's eaten across the region and of course also finds a place on Dolma's menu. But with her expeditions, how does she stay on top of things? 'I've hired women to run the place who know how to cook,' she answers, matter-of-fact, like it's the easiest thing in the world! She says, 'Most women cook the food on our menu in their homes, like sku, paba, thenthuk, chutagi, tamtush and so on. Some recipes I've learnt at the homestays. I have taught and trained our staff operations and service, and now they run the place efficiently without me.'

So, what's next on her radar? 'In the long run, to bring more women into the travel business,' she replies. 'There aren't many women working in travel. I did my basic and advanced mountaineering courses in Darjeeling. In a batch of sixty to eighty people, we were hardly a handful of women. There are many opportunities in this space, and while we do not have a mountaineering institute in Ladakh, we're actively training people at the Ladakh Mountain Guides Association.' Once the said 'season' closes around November in Ladakh, she'll head to either Uttarakhand, Sikkim or Bhutan and return in January for the Chadar trek and the snow leopard trails.

Her travel company is currently run by five women including herself, as she gears up to embark on an expedition to Nun Kun in the Zanskar range. Till date, she has climbed seven glaciers in Ladakh and she's only soaring higher, aiming to complete an international mountaineering course in Nepal. But, somehow, she does not seem driven by money or cut-throat ambition, so I ask her about her opinion on business models and sustainability.

'I grew up in a village where we did not feel the need nor understood the value of money. It felt like a luxury. But today, whatever I do, is to be independent, and to give to others.' Perhaps, it is the resilience of the mountains that she has imbibed. And although she says that she left the mountains and the goats behind, in the pursuit of independence and generosity, she has indeed scaled many peaks.

The Lost Glory

Own Ali Kaizen

Summer has finally arrived in the village of Chiktan, a hamlet situated far off in the town of Kargil in Ladakh. The day is bright and sunny and the stark blue sky is devoid of any clouds today. Like any other day, Mr Kazim reaches his school at ten in the morning. The first thing he does is assemble the kids for morning prayers. The classes for the day are mentioned on a white board; he takes them along with his other colleagues. The timetable has some periods designated for children's games and fun as well. The children seem delighted and happy as they head back to their classrooms, jumping and playing gleefully.

The school is around two kilometres from Mr Kazim's home, which is located near the historical Razi Khar Palace, once a very prominent centre of administration during the reign of king Thata Khan. The palace, which now lies in ruins, has buried within itself many stories pertaining to its dynasty and kingdom; its rise and fall, and how Chiktan went from being the epicentre of a splendid kingdom to an abandoned hamlet. Mr Kazim loves to reminisce about the awe-inspiring stories that surround the palace. At present, he has been entrusted with the responsibilities to improve his school along with his other colleagues. He proudly shares how,

Revival of traditional archery in Nubra Valley

in a short span of time, they have been successful in increasing the enrolment in their school and have also managed to improve the academic and co-curricular performance of their students. It is clear that Mr Kazim is also considered as having considerable knowledge about the history of the heritage and culture of his area. On being asked about the changes and evolution he has seen in his village in terms of the culture and lifestyle, he says promptly, 'a lot'.

He then adds, 'Back in those days, the villages and the people were much more connected and social. People would meet each other very often and they shared an emotional connect with each other.' Describing the society of his times further, he talks about 'Dafangs', the traditional archery festival in Ladakh. 'Dafangs would be the harbinger of summer and the new year where people would come together with joy, play archery games, have a feast at each other's homes following tradition, which now has only become a formality, devoid of any essence it used to have during those times.'

The whole community would participate in the events during Dafangs, irrespective of religion, caste, gender or age. From forming 'zdo', which meant pairs for the game, to the practice of warding off evils through the practice of 'da-rat', where a person would shoot their arrows in all four cardinal directions while reciting various hymns and slogans, the event (Dafangs) was much more than just a festival marking a new season. Choosing the right person for this practice also used to be a task in itself as the person had to remember all the hymns, besides having both parents alive. Drawing a comparison between the archery of the past and the present, he says, 'The bows during those times would be made of deer horns and the arrows were made from the best quality wood fetched from the mountains throughout the past seasons. The arrows were also adorned with the feathers of eagles. Those are now being replaced by the modern ones, which, according to him, do not fill the shooter with the pride and sense of belonging that the old ones did. Even during Dafangs, the use of modern bows and arrows are still not allowed in his village, which is an attempt to keep alive the tradition that was once the pride of his community.

'During the winters, all the people of the village would gather around in one home and distinguished storytellers would be invited. They would expertly engage the villagers for the whole winter so that they could pass the harsh season without much despair. There would be many volumes and episodes of the stories that were based on various themes, rGyalam kesar being one of the voluminous ones,' he says. The storytellers used to be so well-versed with their stories that they would have them all on their fingertips. The traditional way of dressing and how weddings were conducted also seem to have gone through a transformation. Fondly remembering the weddings that he had attended in his childhood, Mr Kazim says, 'The weddings used to be very simple yet elaborate. There would be songs dedicated to each and every thing in the house, be it the inanimate things or the members of the family. The bride, while taking her leave from her home, would address each one of them and recite the designated verses. Those moments were so emotional. The marriages nowadays have no such traditions left.

'These distinct changes may be attributed to the advent of Islam in this part of the land along with rapid modernisation, the signs of which can also be seen in the names and the architecture of the villages. The village called Chortanchan is one such example.

Although, at present the village is wholly Muslim, the name suggests that it once had "chortens", which marks the presence of Buddhism. Later, when Islam arrived, these were gradually demolished and the traditional aspects, including songs, hymns and dances, were gradually weeded out from the newer practices.

'The food and lifestyle have also been influenced in the same way, I don't see the food we used to savour in our childhood. The dishes made from barley and buckwheat, called "paba", are rare these days. If the children eat such food today, they will suffer from an upset stomach the next day.'

As Mr Kazim talks, the school peon also joins in. He agrees with whatever Mr Kazim says and adds, 'Though these days the resources are plenty, happiness has become scarce. We have become more individualistic and greedier.'

Mr Kazim glances at his watch and heads for his next class. The kids greet him, standing up together, saying, 'Good Morning, sir,' in unison.

Credits: Riddhima Khedkar

A Road Map to Empower

Manasi Chokshi

Driving and walking through the city of Leh, one can't help but encounter art in the city—elegantly carved and painted entrance gateways, beautiful circles, sculptures at traffic islands and along highways, art on highway retaining walls, religious patterns and motifs on the pavement, handrails, compound walls, colourful prayer flags, carved prayer drums—all set against a backdrop of the earthy tones of the mountains. The shops and stalls in markets also sell beautiful artefacts in metal, wood and textiles. The religion and heavy inflow of tourists have helped the handicrafts industry blossom here.

The Ladakh handloom and handicrafts department (part of Industries & Commerce, UT Ladakh), is located on the Khardung La road in Leh. The two-floor building has a linear shop frontage, at the centre of which is a gate leading to the office of the department. Padma Chosben, a young and qualified graphic designer working with the department, and Tsering Angdo, an artist, talk about the benefits and efforts taken by the government towards the propagation of the art forms and development of small-scale industries.

Tsering Angdo, wearing a black leather jacket and sunglasses, invites us inside his shop. It is roughly a 150-square-foot shop with ample light but with carved wooden items strewn around like tables, prayer drum handles, beautifully painted entrance portal frames, hundreds of wooden pieces of different sizes, carved pieces and so on. It feels more like a workshop than a shop.

One side of the shop has a mattress with a carved table as a centrepiece. '*Main kaam seekha Thangka painting mai. Abhi kuch 30–35 saal ho gaya mereko iss line main. Tees hazar rupaya jodta hai ek mahine ka. Tax nai deta. Ye toh kya hai uu time ka zamane main, uu saab log socha ki gareeb logo ko upar laane ka. Aisa kaam mila,*' says Tsering in Hindi with a heavy regional accent (I learned the skill of Thangka painting. I have been working in this field for 30–35 years now. I earn a decent Rs 30,000 monthly salary, and I don't have to even pay taxes. Back in those days, the heads and bosses here thought that they needed to give opportunity to the poor and underprivileged, and that is how I landed this job).

Since the handloom and handicraft segment comes under the purview of the Industries Department, Padma talks about the efforts taken by them to achieve their vision. 'Since Ladakh became a Union Territory only in 2019, the department is young, and the work here is in its initial stages and very hectic. The primary agenda of the Industries Department of Ladakh is to encourage entrepreneurship and empower the Ladakhis with self-sustainable occupations.' Counting with her fingers, she says 'We want to encourage the flourishing art forms and help revive the dying ones. To begin with, out of the many arts, we have been focusing on Thangka painting, carpet weaving, knitting, wood carving, silver filigree, Papu (shoe) making and felting. They take sheep wool washed and beaten into a carpet, and then they do embroidery—it's a traditional form of carpet weaving. Felting—sheep wool washed and beaten into carpet form—then they do embroidery, the traditional form of carpet weaving.'

'Every year we get requests from several villages from the Leh district to conduct training programmes for men and women who are looking for employment and are willing to learn the craft. After an initial survey and supervision of the village and villagers, we hired and deputed an art instructor to train them. Depending on the art form, the training may span from six months up to two years. The department provides for the raw materials, machinery and a stipend for the villagers. The villagers simply come and learn the craft. There are challenges there as well. Not everyone who enrols in our training programmes becomes successful. Some drop out, some have family issues, and there is not much discipline in the people here to work outside of home.'

Tsering Angdo is one such villager from Thikse who participated in a similar programme some thirty years ago when it was under the Jammu and Kashmir administration. He learned the skill of Thangka painting but moved to paint carved wooden artefacts, because it is faster and easier to paint wooden surfaces. The wooden artefacts he decorates are primarily for homes, like prayer chairs, prayer book covers, home temple entrance doors, prayer drum handles, almirahs for the home temples, etc. He shows photographs of more work he has done before. Some pieces are rated at over Rs 1,00,000. The vibrant colours, delicate colouring, shading technique, and clarity of the motifs in all the artefacts are fascinating. To expose this art to the outside world and to continue to be relevant in modern times, the department runs an incubation centre near the Leh Gate and a showroom by the name 'Brand Ladakh' at the Leh Market. The incubation centre helps the artists learn sales, marketing, branding, graphic design, photography, social media, packaging, etc. It helps them understand market demands and gives them a platform to display and sell their artwork.

For a larger reach within the country, the department participates in exhibition-cum-sale expos. Padma explains, 'One of the successful models we have implemented is "Enchanting Ladakh" in Delhi. It is a two-week expo in Dilli Haat, dedicated to the arts, crafts, cuisine and performances of Ladakh. We select ninety artisans based on skill and product quality from all art forms under the handicraft, handloom and food processing departments. The artists' travel, lodging, boarding, stall cost and stall decoration are all paid for by the department. The artists only have to go and sell. The money they make is theirs. We participate in similar expos at the India International Trade Fair, Mumbai International Trade Expo, Uttar Pradesh Trade Expo and many others all over the country. Since the department is only three years old, we have to hold their hands through the process. But the longer-term goal is to eventually make them independent.

'They also organise workshops for art institutes like the National Institute of Design, the National Institute of Fashion Technology, and other institutes throughout the country. In this model, the students from other parts of the country come to Leh for a month or two, to learn and practise the respective art forms. The training centres are distributed in the district of Leh where the art form can be learned. That way, it promotes conscious tourism and also helps the economy.'

Though the Union Territory of Ladakh is undertaking sizable measures towards handicrafts and handlooms, enabling the growth of small-scale industries for and by the Ladakhis is challenging. Government jobs continue to hold a higher ground in the psyche of the people due to job security. The challenges aren't made any easier by the inhospitable terrain, harsh climate, eco-sensitive zones, sparse population density, lack of entrepreneurship, limited infrastructure and temporary population of tourists and migrant entrepreneurs. However, the commitment and willingness of employees like Padma to uplift her people are endearing. Padma is a local from Chuchot and a design graduate from National Institute of Fashion Technology (NIFT), Delhi. Her young mind is very aware of all the workings of the department. The conscious effort of the department to hire the local youth is a commendable foresight that someday will empower and encourage holistic growth in Ladakh.

Amchis: The Green Healers

Saylee Soundalgekar

You don't see large trees and shrubs in Ladakh,
The mountain seems bare,
The rocks sharp enough to pierce,
The men, walking for miles together, indefinitely...

But tiptoe on the land and breathe slowly.

At every footstep, you will find ABUNDANCE.
Where you step there is the moss that cures,
What you plucked has aromas that heal,
Who smiled at you was the amchi of the village.

Amchis are protectors of the forest, messengers of traditional indigenous wisdom, and pioneers of the Sowa Rigpa system; they are one of the locals of the Trans-Himalayan region. Sowa Rigpa is derived from the Mongolian word 'Am-rjay', which means 'superior to all'. It is commonly known as the Tibetan system of medicine, and its practitioner is called the Amchi. The Sowa Rigpa system of medicine is also the traditional medicine system of Tibet, Mongolia, Bhutan, China, Nepal, Bhuriat, Russia, and the Himalayan areas of Himachal Pradesh, Arunachal Pradesh, Darjeeling and Sikkim in India.

'You have to complete a rigorous training process, and practise for a minimum of five years to be recognised as an Amchi,' says Dr Sonam Dawa. 'Amchis never ask for costs and services. It all depends on the people to present something besides money. Traditionally, they were thanked with wheat or barley; or we helped the Amchi family during the harvest.'

'You have to walk in the forest, understand seasons and biodiversity and have the urge to bring about a socio-medical change. There are tens of thousands of villages in Ladakh, and each one of the villages has an Amchi. They are the only community allowed to venture into the reserved forested land. With an average of four months of growing season, they go into the sacred forest, worship and apologise to the tree for hurting it, and bring the medicines. Even today over 60 per cent of Ladakhis trust the Amchis and *Gyuchi* (book of Sowa Rigpa medicines) more than modern medicine, as the healers and medicines are rooted in our land.'

Dr Sonam Dawa is based in Leh City. 'Look here!' he says, as he walks across a half-an-acre fruit orchard laden with apple and apricot blossoms. 'We use no pesticides, no additives to the soil, making apples and apricots of the best quality.' Dr Sonam Dawa is the first PhD holder in Floriculture and Landscape Architecture from Ladakh region and is now working as a Horticulture Development Officer with the Horticulture Department, UT Ladakh. He graduated from University of Agricultural Sciences, Bengaluru and did his postgraduation and PhD from SKUAST-Kashmir University.

He says, 'I realised that we Ladakhis are different. To begin, I never knew soil can be manipulated using materials other than animal and plant produce until I stepped out of Ladakh. Secondly, thanks to the Silk Route and natural land fertility, we are a community of fulfilled, wealthy people.'

Every traditional household in Leh used to be self-sustained. Growing food and rearing animals for self-consumption, the homes have acres of land growing barley, buckwheat, vegetables, potatoes and medicinal herbs.

It is almost impossible to get cow milk, yak milk, the local alcohol 'chang', and freshly grown vegetables in the local market. 'Not because we don't want tourists to share, but because we prepare it solely for the household, hence we have limited quantity. Most of us have forgotten what it is to be self-sufficient.'

'Fermented products, packed food and tetrapacks have taken over the market. Tourism with homestays and rented motorbikes have given us easy money. National and international natural medicine brands have approached the Ministry with a demand for herbs and rare medicines. We have refused to supply to any clients that demand mass production with synthetic methods of growing plants. The short growing seasons maintain a single crop pattern, soil fertility and exclusivity to the medicines.'

Dawa walks in his experimental garden with dandelions and Russian box shrubs. 'Russian box thorns are camel food. The double-humped camels, you know! The ones that are found in Nubra. Ladakh is now an exporter of seabuckthorn.' Being certified in Sowa Rigpa himself, Dr Dawa has documented over

300 medical florae in the state with their local names, botanical names, Sowa Rigpa names, and Sowa Rigpa medicinal use, family, habitat and botanical features.

'I have just returned from Nubra,' he said. 'They called me there to examine the apricots. They are not flowering. They seem to be inflicted with worms. There is no sunshine, no dryness in the air. It is the first time in the history of over forty-five years that I have not seen summer!'

Leh, in the year 2023, had skipped summer. From chilly winters, the district has moved on to become a rainfall region.

Number-crunching Nun

Manasi Chokshi

Amidst the hordes of tourists, Buddhist monks and nuns are hard to miss. Fully robed, in plain maroon and saffron colours, tonsured, sneaker-wearing, backpack-carrying, they are often spotted in their day-to-day domestic activities like shopping, reading and travelling.

In popular understanding, monks and nuns are individuals that have renounced domestic life and all the pleasures that come with it; they are expected to lead a life without involvement of and interaction with society. One wonders how the ascetics of Ladakh lead a 'normal' life?

Jigmat Lhazes, a nun and a qualified Sowa Rigpa practitioner, helps us understand the nuances of the Buddhist ascetic life in Leh: 'I belong to the nomadic community from a small village in Kharnak, near the Tanglang La pass, a hundred kilometres south of the city of Leh. Being a very curious child, I was very regular at the village monastery and developed a keen interest in Buddhism and spirituality very early in life. I wanted to pursue it further. After some convincing, my parents spoke to the Ringpoche there, and I was initiated as a nun in the year 2000 at the age of ten. I

Credits: Mintana Palkar

was the eldest daughter, and I continued to live with my parents. I helped around with the family chores and responsibilities. After a couple of years, my aunt, also a nun, wrote to my father about the Ladakh Nuns' Association (LNA) at Leh. And thus, I was enrolled at LNA for my formal and spiritual education. Ladakh Nuns' Association is also where I live currently. My education is from Leh—the Lamdon School till my tenth grade, junior college from science in Government Higher Secondary School, and Bachelor of Sowa Rigpa Medicine and Surgery (BSRMS) from Central Institute for Buddhist Studies (CIBS).'

Just like in other cultures, it is a matter of great pride if a family member surrenders oneself to religion or attains monkhood. While Ladakh was under monarchy, a prince of the royal family had to be dedicated to Buddhism. The royal families were also primary patrons of monasteries back then. Hence, Ladakh is dotted with several monasteries and nunneries.

The LNA was established in 1996. It is an NGO that provides opportunities to young girls whose families may experience difficulties to provide for secular and monastic education. It is a nunnery run under the moral and spiritual care of older nuns. To promote the role of nuns, LNA encourages them to pursue basic and higher education in Buddhist philosophy and in traditional Tibetan medical studies. It also runs orientation programmes, charities and seminars for locals, foreigners and Indian tourists.

Describing her routine, Jigmat says, 'At LNA, my day typically starts early with chanting and prayers. I then do some chores at the nunnery, go to work and end the day at the nunnery with some chores, rituals, chanting, and prayers. There are other senior

Sowa Rigpa practitioners, or Amchis, at the nunnery as well. As part of the chores, we help other nuns heal, nurture, and take care of them when they're unwell. We also participate in and conduct religious and non-religious workshops, training sessions, discourses, seminars and things like that.'

Sowa Rigpa is the indigenous knowledge system of Ladakh, where the healing is done by a range of therapies like medicinal herbs, acupuncture, vacuum cups, herbal oils, panchkarma, and so on.

Sowa Rigpa is identified and promoted by the Ministry of Ayush and also offers BSRMS, a six-year, full time undergraduate course that trains individuals to be qualified medical practitioners. The course is offered by six institutes in cities like Bengaluru, Sikkim, Darjeeling, Varanasi, and two in Leh.

Jigmat works as a data entry specialist in the research department of one such research institute and medical facility, The National Institute of Sowa Rigpa (NISR). The campus is located near the Leh airport. It has three buildings: one dedicated to teaching, one to research and administration, and one to the OPD, panchakarma kriya and massage. Jigmat's department conducts research on herbs, documents them and applies for patents for the herbal medicine at the institute. Her work cubicle has six other staff members, with walls pasted with posters of medicinal plants, their benefits, photographs and scientific names. Some areas of the office also display banners with treatments offered at the centre.

On enquiring about the benefits of Sowa Rigpa, Jigmat explains, 'I have a patient from New Delhi who has completely stopped consuming allopathic medicines. The Sowa Rigpa technique has suited her the best. We get patients from India and abroad, for stomach ulcers, arthritis, cervical issues, migraines, hepatitis, etc. In fact, I have switched to consuming only Sowa Rigpa medicines after learning about the ill-effects of antibiotics and allopathy. Ladakhis prefer only the Sowa Rigpa medications, so much that even the primary health care centres have Amchis.'

Clad in a maroon robe and sweatshirt, wearing sneakers, black-rimmed spectacles and a wide smile, Jigmat has a comforting presence. On asking her about the role of spirituality in her life, she says, 'There are many ways to follow the path, you could choose any of them—Mahayana, Vajrayana, Mahabodhi, Hinayana, Vipassana—it doesn't matter; all lead to Dharma. Most monks and nuns live as a sangha or a community and that is why there are so many monasteries and nunneries in the region. Alternatively, you may find monks living away from the sangha. That is also accepted. As a monk or nun, one must live away from the family, dedicate time to learning the spiritual and religious practices. We can do other jobs and work as per our interest but there aren't a lot of restrictions on the extent or depth of involvement in the religion.

'From personal experience and observing people around, the fast-changing life is affecting peoples' mental health. The Dharma and spirituality help me there. I have also done a couple Vipassana meditation courses—there is a centre here in Leh. The technique helps me stay sane in times of distress.'

Jigmat is ambitious and committed to learning new things. She has been taking up online courses, learning about computers, software and things like that. She is looking forward to pursuing a master's degree in philosophy or psychology, and later a PhD. She mentions that this will help her counsel, teach and heal her patients holistically. Equipped with the qualification of a medical practitioner and the wisdom of a nun, Jigmat truly embodies how education and spirituality can empower one's life, which can, in turn, help society.

From her experiences, one can say that Buddhist monks and nuns lead normal lives of balancing chores at the monasteries and nunneries along with studying, working and pursuing their passions. Their monasteries and nunneries are amidst the city, with access to all amenities, exposure to the world and, most importantly, allowance to pursue a formal education. The perception that ascetics are to lead restricted lives in solitude, or can only have the most basic essentials, is completely flipped when one encounters monks and nuns in Ladakh. It reflects the evolving, liberal and diverse culture of Ladakh where an ascetic also has a place in conventional society.

In Pursuit of That Perfect Apricot

Ruma Pratihar

If there's one thing that's almost constant throughout Ladakh, it is the apricot. The trees dot almost every property, growing abundantly, like orange jewels hanging off their green canopies. In Leh they are sweet like jam, especially those that have just fallen off their tree. They just need a wipe (or two) before you can eat them. You see, even the dirt in most parts of Ladakh is cleaner than the air I breathe in my city. In the quest to find the perfect apricots to take back home, I learnt two things: the first being that big ideas and dreams can be achieved with simplicity and often require little to get started; the second is that the vendors from Aryan Valley (near the Tibetan Street Market) perhaps sell the best dried apricots in Leh.

I was led to the first realisation by a gentleman who asked me to visit a little store near the Leh Market to buy some apricots to take back home. The signboard outside the shop was rather upfront: they offered laundry, paid water filling facilities and seasonal organic produce. Apricots, local capers, apples, saffron, some berries, dried chamomile flowers, sun-dried tomatoes, jams and spreads lined the shelves alongside apricot kernel oil and tsampa packages (all packed in glass and paper, with little or no plastic).

Credits: Subin Selva

Credits: Subin Selva

These were flanked by a bookshelf with old and new books. Some cotton laundry bags were also on sale, and at the entrance was a table with options of fresh apricots and sea buckthorn juice. It was a dreamy space with foraged flowers adorning tables, the wood-decked interiors, and a water-filling station that lets you buy clean drinking water at throwaway prices. The only catch—bring your own bottle!

Sonam Dorje started the shop to literally clean up the mess generated by industries. 'When we grew up, the air, water and earth was much cleaner; but with development, I am seeing things getting out of hand,' he says, indicating the growing pollution and increasing carbon footprint of local enterprises. He is keen to undo the damage that has been inflicted, bring back the greener Ladakh, make its air breathable and the water clean again. Sonam currently runs his farm at Suspol with a team and a shop where they sell its produce.

What about the business model, and whether he can sustain the aspiration through his store, I ask him. 'This is a lifestyle model, and so far, we have sustained it. And if humanity wants to survive, initiatives like mine will have to be sustained.' With a smile, he continues, 'I have no superpower, I am just doing my bit; improving the quality of our food, making it edible once again. I aim to enhance the quality of our food, making it enjoyable once more. Similarly, I strive to improve the quality of air, water and land in my own small way. While I may not have the means to make grand changes, I choose not to sit idly. Instead, I contribute with my humble efforts wherever possible.'

It is seven in the evening, and the shop is packed with tourists and locals alike; it's time for the laundry pick-ups. And before I know it, the apricots are all gone. I quickly pack some jam and scurry towards the market to look for the second-best option. On the road that connects the bustling market square with the bus stop, further ahead is a narrow but colourful stretch with vendors from the Aryan Valley. Here, I meet Ajang Tashi Namgail from Darchik, belonging to the ethnic group of Brokpas in Ladakh. He has some dried berries, a ton of walnuts and myriad types of apricots. 'There are four kinds of apricots, but right here, this one, is the best you will ever eat in your life,' he asserts. He conjures a bag from behind him and offers me a dried apricot. It's fleshy, soft and sweet, with a tiny brittle seed.

Although he speaks like a seasoned salesman, his words come from a place of pride, not exaggeration: 'The Aryan Valley khubanis (apricot) are bigger and sweeter than anywhere else in Ladakh. If you are impressed by the apricot, you should try our grapes in October. It's our water, it's magical. It is not filtered, and we don't use fertilisers either.'

In that twilight hour, I mentally laughed (and wept a little) at this irony of pride and peril. Ajang, clearly far removed from the environmental struggles of Sonam, took pride in the simplicity of his trade and produce. Yet, he lived in exactly the same magical world that Sonam aspired to preserve, if not bring it back entirely. On that note, I asked Ajang about the cashews that lay next to the apricots. 'Oh, those…they come from Goa,' he chuckled, leaving me equal parts confused and amused!

Paba shorba

Khambir dantur

A Platter-full

Own Ali Kaizen

We are all introduced to different kinds of food over our lives. I was first introduced to paba-tSamik when I was seven years old. I visited my Apo-Abilay (Nana-Nani: maternal grandparents) during one of my vacations, which used to be a customary visit. It was a sunny day, and the sun had just passed overhead when Abilay (Nana: maternal grandfather) came to my Apo's (Nani: maternal grandmother) workplace, carrying what looked like food of some sort. She knew I would be there too, because staying outdoors used to be my favourite pastime. Grandpa's workplace, as one could imagine, was not a fancy office with revolving chairs. It was a nice cosy place under the shade of an apricot tree just a couple of yards away from their home. A stream flowed nearby, making a gentle gushing sound to which my Apo would often fall asleep after lunch. There were some flat boulders around the place which would come in handy for them to 'sun-dry' the apricots during the late apricot seasons.

Apo was a person with soft hands who could mould anything and could make anything out of scraps. From local agricultural tools like khem, tokchey, tSelbu to more complex items like thab, he had made it all. Now, when my Abilay came with the bowls of food, I was overjoyed because I was already hungry. After much anticipation, as I finally hopped onto those bowls to relish my favourite rTsab-khur, my joy turned into dismay; there was some other food instead of what I had hoped for.

I went to Apo and told him that I didn't want to eat the paba as I really wanted to eat rTsab-khur instead. But he and Abilay convinced me to have a lump of the paba-tSamik first and then decide for myself whether to eat more of it or not. They were confident that I'd love this cuisine as much as I loved rTsab.

'What is it?' I asked them.

'Paba-tSamik,' they explained. 'Paba, made generally from barley flour and sophisticatedly from buckwheat flour; tSamik, prepared from a mixture of curd, coriander, lentil, methi, etc.' The blend of these two was so delicious that I eventually savoured it from the heart.

Today, this cuisine is seldom served in Ladakh for many reasons. Firstly, because rice and wheat have replaced almost every other food as a staple option. Second, paba, made out of barley, is considered to be a heavy dish. In today's health-conscious society, people often choose low-carb food over these, which are very high in calories. But, having said that, in the far-off places of Ladakh, where people still very much rely on agriculture, paba thukpa, paba tsamik and paba dangthur are very common dishes. It is believed that the buckwheat, grown in only some specific pockets of Ladakh, has anti-bacterial and anti-carcinogenic effects, not to mention the positive effects of other Himalayan herbs that are used in the making of these cuisines.

We also encounter food that we now see everywhere, but each place has its own variant of it. Momos, for example, can be found everywhere in Northern India, and in fact, all over the world, from stalls to restaurants. Fancy restaurants have also found their way to put momo-inspired cuisines in their menu lists. If we trace the root of this commonly served delicacy, we reach mok-moks, in the valleys of Tibet. With the changing times and due to political, cultural and temporal reasons, this cuisine travelled across Asia. When China attacked Tibet in the 1950s, the Tibetans fled to many parts of India like Ladakh, Dharamshala, Darjeeling, Delhi, etc. As they came, they brought their culinary traditions along. The distinct cultures and heritages had a confluence and then evolved gradually with time.

Mok-moks too had their fair share of evolution. Originally it would be stuffed with mutton or other meaty chunks. With time, many versions of it, like paneer momos, veg momos and fried momos made their way into the popular food culture of India. Not only the endless flavours and tastes but mok-moks also started to be served in many forms and shapes. Some like to savour it with thukpa as mok-mok-thukpa mix, others like it served solely with spicy chutney. Some like it steamed and others love them fried and crunchy.

Mok-moks, as most of the Ladakhis call them, are relatively bigger and massy with perfect crescent-shaped shells. In mainland India, they get smaller in size with a very thin shell. The name also changes subtly, from 'mok-mok' to 'mo-mo'. Apart from these, Ladakh is heaven for many more exquisite foods. Cuisines like chu-tagi, sKyu, prapu are some variants that, in appearance, might seem like pasta or noodles, but their flavour and taste differ totally from what we find in other places. When Ladakh was cut off from the rest of the world, these indigenous foods, which heavily depended on their own produce at home, were its people's sole source of energy. Now, like any other place in the world, Ladakh is facing the consequences of fast-paced growth, being overwhelmed by the outpouring numbers of tourists on one side and fast-paced urbanisation on the other.

It is becoming more prone to assimilation of its culture and heritage. The food, the language and the culture are being diluted day by day, and the younger generations are being dragged further and further away from their roots. However, all is not lost. One silver lining that we see amidst the slowly diluting food culture of Ladakh is the mamani. A traditional ethnic food carnival observed in winters, Mamani is now being celebrated with utmost fervour all over Ladakh, across religions. I remember going to my Nani's place especially for the mamani as she would make the best rTsab khur blended with apricot oil. I'd also get plenty of dried apricots and walnuts. After stocking them in a bag, I'd come home the next day, happy and eager to show off my stock of food to my siblings. They'd then often exchange their bakery biscuits with some of my walnuts. Mamani, along with a food carnival, also serves as a day when the people remember their ancestors and honour them. We offer prayers and food to them, with a hope that our culture lives long and is cherished by the generations to come.

Marathon Story

Ruma Pratihar

For most runners, the Ladakh Marathon is a pilgrimage. Weeks, and often even months, before the actual run, it sees runners from across the world trickling into the city. During the month of the marathon, if you can spot the tourists navigating their way, you'll also see a quiet runner sprinting or walking at a regulated speed, nodding and acknowledging a fellow runner when they cross paths. Why do they run? What propels them, forward and onward, even upward, in the case of terrains like Leh? For Priyansh Rai, a native of Bhopal who is currently residing in Bengaluru, the Ladakh Marathon is important.

'I've been running for 15 years,' he says. 'I keep challenging myself. Having completed many marathons, and knowing Ladakh, I knew it would be quite the test of my endurance.' He arrived in Leh three weeks before the marathon to prepare for the big day, the tenth edition of Ladakh Marathon, in September 2023.

'There's always a reason why someone takes to running. When we meet strangers in a new land, one may not always initiate conversations. But when we meet another runner, there is automatically a connection, a curiosity to learn their story and share your own. You get to see

how you are placed in those stories. That's the magic. But there is no comparison or competition, only learning. The only competition is you versus yourself.'

For Priyansh, the competition was indeed with himself, trying to outdo his best, 4 hours and 43 minutes at the full marathon (slightly over 42 kilometres) in Dubai. But he finished in five hours. 'The last 7-8 kilometres were difficult and the stretch was completely uphill,' he explains. And indeed, the Ladakh Marathon is the highest and one of the toughest in the world. Started in 2012, following the 2010 flash floods, the marathon aimed at offering a platform to the Ladakhi youth and also put Ladakh on the world map, making it a coveted milestone achievement for runners all across the world. This was exactly what caught Raj Hosali's attention during another marathon in another city.

'At one of the marathons, I saw someone wearing a T-shirt that read "world's highest marathon" and I knew it was something I had to do. I live in Delhi and Leh is not very far for me.' He had started running by virtue of a fitness challenge during COVID-19. He visited Ladakh for the first time just a month before the marathon, on a family trip followed by the run in September.

Priyansh had his first tryst with the land of high passes in 2016 as a tourist. Smitten by not just the beauty but also the effect it had on his physical being, he states, 'I was already a runner, but Ladakh is a leveller—it tests everyone in the same manner. It does not matter where you come from or how fit you are. The low oxygen levels impact the body so adversely that you couldn't even climb a floor without struggling. I saw people being hospitalised, and some even being compelled to leave Leh overnight.'

Like all tourists, Khardung La was also on his agenda, where he observed people cycling and even running at one of the world's highest motorable roads. 'I was so stunned when I saw these people while we were running out of breath just walking till the bathroom! This made me want to attempt it,' he says. 'And it's not just the low oxygen; the temperature changes very fast. At one moment it's cold, the next minute the sun will make it 40 degrees. So, the body has to adapt, and the recovery time is longer. You have to observe your body and re-engineer its devices. No matter how much you prepare, what happens at ground zero cannot be anticipated or predicted.'

They began in the wee hours of the mornings, waking up at 2 a.m. to start the run by 6 a.m. for the full marathon, the temperature at that time ranging between 7–9 degrees. Their 42-kilometre route began from the NDS Memorial Stadium following the Leh–Manali Highway tracing the Indus river alongside the Stok range of mountains. 'It was a great start; I am assuming there were more than 2,000 participants. After 8–9 kilometres, people began dispersing, finding their own pace. You are then on your own, with the picturesque trail for company. The Leh–Manali Highway was shut; people had come out from their homes, some in traditional attire, playing instruments, cheering runners.'

Raj, too, found his joy in the clean air and the lack of pollution and vehicles. But the best part, he asserts, are the people. 'Unlike other marathons, you are mandated to arrive in Leh a week before the run. The entire city is filled with runners. Every restaurant you visit, you will bump into someone you met at a previous run. And because you're staying longer in the city, you also make friends and keep in constant touch.'

Around the same time, although it began a few hours before, at around 3 a.m., was the Khardung La Challenge, a 72-kilometre route, also called the Ultra Marathon, one of the toughest runs that begins at 13,000 ft peaking to over 17,000 ft. Here, Somu, originally from Bengaluru, and having completed quite a few Ultra Challenges down south, had embarked on the challenge during his maiden trip to Ladakh! Which, for those who know, is perhaps the biggest gamble almost bordering on whimsy.

'I had heard about the Ladakh marathons from my fellow runners. I've always wanted to see the place, but investing as much money in the stay and travel from Bengaluru did not seem practical. I submitted my application (essentially previous marathon records) and even got qualified,' says the man who is also a badminton player. Somu found joy (and a way to stay fit) with running when badminton courts had shut down during COVID-19.

'So,' he says, 'I started running and enjoying travelling to different places. I liked the change in terrains and landscapes, since I found running between buildings in Bengaluru boring! I eventually decided to do the Ultra in Ladakh because I always wanted to see the place. I arrived two weeks ago and went to places like Pangong Lake and Nubra Valley. I would run every morning to prepare myself for the big day. I did not enjoy the car drive as much as I enjoyed running in these lovely locations,' he laughs nonchalantly.

Attempting the same route was Mrunalini, who is neither new to Ladakh nor to the concept of running in its treacherous terrain. This is her fifth visit, the first being in 2010: a road trip from Pune with her husband. She and her husband ran their half marathon before COVID-19 and then secured a silver medal in the next two years. 'It was at that moment that my husband and I decided to train for the Ultra,' she says. But as fate would have it, her husband suffered a stroke and passed away. 'It was our combined dream to run this marathon, and I have come back to honour his memory,' she says. But Ladakh is also intermingled with other memories for Mrunalini. 'I like it for the people. During my many trips, I have made friends from all across the valleys. I love the barren beauty, the deserts and everything about it.'

Priyansh also fell in love with the place, in a new way. 'I first came as a tourist, with an itinerary. But in these twenty-one days, there was no agenda. I discovered local cuisine, walked the same route, and trekked to Namgyal Tsemo monastery every day. I absorbed the details.' In the end, the literal end, the land holds a special place for each, where dreams are tested and memories are made, one marathon at a time.

My Culture, My Heritage

Dr Sonam Wangchuk

The Himalayan Cultural Heritage Foundation (HCHF) is a community-based organisation devoted to promoting and conserving the indigenous, natural, and historic heritage of the Himalayas by working directly with the different mountain communities and strengthening and supporting community-based institutions. The foundation places great stress on training programmes and workshops that ensure more practical and beneficial outcomes, both in terms of learning and preserving the rich cultural heritage of the region. The promotion and preservation activities include cultural and natural heritage, art and crafts skills, folk traditions, community-based management of cultural and natural resources, and language and literature. Another important aim is to encourage scientific research and documentation of the impact of climate change on these mountain cultures. This knowledge, we believe, will propel the development of sustainable solutions to mitigate its degradation. The HCHF programmes are carried out in Ladakh and other regions of the Himalayas.

Ladakh is famous for its moveable and immoveable heritage, like ancient temples, wall paintings, wooden carvings, ancient paintings, manuscripts, metal images, textiles, paper drawings, block prints and so on. Monument conservation, especially Buddhist stupas and wall paintings, is one of the core activities that the HCHF started and has gained momentum over the years.

Credits: Jiten Desai

The Himalayan Cultural Heritage Foundation has successfully completed four major ancient wall painting conservation projects in Sumda Chun Stupa (Leh), Takkhung Khawoche (Cave Temple, Leh), Chomophu Temple (Nubra), and Bodh Kharbu Monastery (Kargil). The Himalayan Cultural Heritage Foundation has also restored more than fifty old stupas across various villages in Ladakh.

Credits: Himalayan Cultural Heritage Foundation (HCHF)

Stupa restoration in Chemdey village

Painting conservation inside a stupa in Sumdha Chun village

Stupa restoration in Chushul village, Changthang

In 2018, the HCHF took up the task of illuminating a much-talked-about yet equally neglected part of our history, the Silk Route. A programme named 'Silk Route Initiative Ladakh' was conceived to revive and strengthen the intangible heritage associated with the famous Silk Route and its legacy. Under this programme, the HCHF has also been supporting the Mamani Festival in Kargil and the Saichen Folk Festival in Nubra. Through these festivals, several traditional dances, songs, handicrafts, ethnic foods, and traditional sports, such as archery, are being revived and promoted.

Credits: Himalayan Cultural Heritage Foundation (HCHF)

Participation by women's groups (both Muslim and Buddhist) at the Mamani Ethnic Food Festival in Kargil

Traditional dance during a festival in Nubra

Credits: Himalayan Cultural Heritage Foundation (HCHF)

Revival of monastic arts, crafts and rituals in Chemdey Gonpa

Credits: Himalayan Cultural Heritage Foundation (HCHF)

Cultivation of medicinal herbs in Nubra

A workshop on stone carving of mantras

A basket weaving workshop in Nubra

Credits: Himalayan Cultural Heritage Foundation (HCHF)

The Himalayan Cultural Heritage Foundation has identified a small village called Rongdo in the Nubra Valley to cultivate medicinal plants under the direction and expertise of Amchi Lobsang Tsultrim. The villagers are encouraged to cultivate different medicinal plants in their home gardens and fields. The collected medicinal plants are given, free of charge, to local Amchis (traditional doctors) who prepare medicines for the benefit of patients.

Credits: Himalayan Cultural Heritage Foundation (HCHF)

Cultivation of medicinal herbs in Nubra

Cultivation of medicinal herbs in Nubra

Cultivation of medicinal herbs in Nubra

The Rock Art Unit (RAU) was established under the aegis of the HCHF to bring focused attention to the research, conservation and documentation of rock arts in Ladakh. The convenor of the RAU, Mr Tashi Ldawa Thsangspa, is the local pioneer of rock art research, and he is assisted by the co-convenor, Mr Viraf Mehta, a Delhi-based social anthropologist who has been documenting the rock arts of Ladakh since 2009. The Ladakh Rock Art Resource Centre, dedicated to research and preservation of rock arts in Ladakh and other Himalayan regions, was established in Leh in 2021. It has the rarest collection of books on Ladakh, rock arts, and other regions. Interactive sessions for researchers, scholars, and students are also hosted.

Credits: Himalayan Cultural Heritage Foundation (HCHF)

Petroglyph at Dhomkhar Dho

An awareness programme organised in Saboo village

Credits: Himalayan Cultural Heritage Foundation (HCHF)

An awareness programme and training workshop in Kubet village, Nubra

Credits: Himalayan Cultural Heritage Foundation

Under the My Culture, My Heritage project, several heritage education and awareness programmes are being conducted. Under this project, the youth get a chance to reflect on and get acquainted with their socio-cultural tangible and intangible histories. They also contribute through writeups and their views and concerns about their culture and heritage. Their articles are published in the heritage magazine *Heritage Himalaya*.

About the Guest Contributors

Dr Sonam Wangchuk

Dr Sonam Wangchuk is the founder of the Himalayan Cultural Heritage Foundation (HCHF), an NGO working in the field of conservation and preservation of indigenous cultural and natural heritage in Ladakh. He is the editor of *Heritage Himalaya*, a biannual heritage magazine dedicated to the heritage of the Himalayas. He is president of the Ladakh Cultural Forum (LCF), and also served as president of the International Association for Ladakh Studies (IALS) from 2015 to 2023. He has several publications and paper presentations to his credit at both the national and international levels. Besides these, he is also involved with other national and international organisations as a project consultant. (sonamleh2@gmail.com)

Dr Ghulam Mehdi

Dr Ghulam Mehdi is a sociology lecturer in the Education Department of the Union Territory of Ladakh. Dr Mehdi, hailing from Tyakshi village in Turtuk block, which became part of India following the 1971 Indo–Pak War, holds an MA and a PhD in sociology from the University of Jammu, and has also qualified NTA-UGC NET in sociology. His dissertation is titled, *Tribe in Transition—A Study of Habitat, Economy, and Society of the Baltis of Ladakh*. (gmghmehdi@gmail.com)

Sunetro Ghosal

Sunetro Ghosal is an independent interdisciplinary researcher with an interest in human–nature interactions. He is also the editor of the Ladakh-based periodical, *Stawa*, and the journal *Ladakh Studies*. (sunetro@stawa.org)

About the Contributors

Photography

Subin Selva

Subin is the principal architect and photographer at The Grid Studio, Mumbai. With an eye for detail, flare for design and lighting, he brings about the best of the built environments. He has undertaken professional architecture and interior photo shoots for Central Railways, Gauri Khan Designs, The Leela, Talathy Panthaky Architects, and a number of other interior and architectural designers. (subin@thegridstudio.in)

Jiten Desai

Jiten is an architect with over eleven years of experience in the field and has worked extensively in Conservation Architecture. Over the course of his career, he has worked on projects of various degrees and types across the country ranging from site documentation works to preparing and getting projects executed onsite. He has also won two UNESCO Asia-Pacific Awards and a HUDCO Design Award. He has currently set up his independent architectural firm TeamARC in 2018. He is presently working on conservation projects in Maharashtra. (teamarc.jd@gmail.com)

Authors

Manasi Chokshi

An architect by qualification and teacher by heart, Manasi is passionate about history, indology, research and writing. She has contributed to several books by the People Place Project and has published articles in research journals and books on architecture. Currently a core faculty member at one of Mumbai's leading architecture institutes, she has also been recipient of the MASA Best Teacher Award 2019. She runs a design practice, 'The Grid Studio', with her architect and photographer husband Subin Selva. (manasichokshi@gmail.com)

Jigmet Lhazes

Jigmet is a nun from Kharnak village situated in Changthang in Ladakh. She did her high school at Lamdon Model Senior Secondary, Leh, and higher secondary school at Government Boys Higher Secondary, Leh. After that, she did Bachelor of Sowa Rigpa Medicine and Surgery (BSRMS) at the Central Institute of Buddhist Studies (CIBS), Choglamsar, Leh–Ladakh. After completion, she worked as a Project Associate-1 in CSIR-Traditional Medicine Digital Library (TKDL). She is currently working as an assistant professor in CIBS, Choglamsar, Leh–Ladakh. (jigmetlhazes2@gmail.com)

Nidhi Dhingra

Nidhi has over fifteen years of experience in research writing, and on all things travel, history and culture. With a firm foothold in publishing, she has led over thirty projects exploring India with *Goodearth Publications*; contributed with experiential features to *National Geographic*, *RoundGlass Sustain*, *LiveMint*, and has also dabbled with childrens' literature. A people person, she thrives on community interactions and has a keen bent towards stories of impact and sustainability. Forever on the move, she travels with a curious mind, a sketchpad and her taste buds, discovering various treasures and illustrating them on the go.
(nidhi.dhingra10@gmail.com)

Own Ali Kaizen

Born and raised in a small village of Kargil district in Ladakh, Own did his schooling from the Navodaya Vidyalaya in Kargil before moving out to pursue further studies. After completing a bachelor's degree in zoological science from the University of Delhi, he went to Punjab and did his master's in human genetics. Currently, he is studying anthropology besides working on some other projects. His interests include poetry, hiking and storytelling.
(ownalikz9@gmail.com)

Rashida Kousar (Kalikhan)

Rashida is a current anthropology postgraduate and runs a cafe (traditional kitchen Lonpo House in Leh). (rashidakalikhan@gmail.com)

Riddhima Khedkar

An architect, urban designer and academician by profession, Riddhima had the pleasure of studying in Mumbai, New York City and Weimar. She is passionate about art, modern architecture, travelling, writing, research, painting, photography and baking. Her research focuses on the socio-cultural aspect of cities where she is curious about exploring the symbiotic and asymbiotic relationship between the built and unbuilt. (riddhimakhedkar@gmail.com)

Ruma Pratihar

Her pen name is dedicated to a woman who has been her first teacher and biggest inspiration. Ruma has worked with some prestigious brands and people in the past. The People Place Project is key to her success, a landmark in her career, and she continues to be her strongest pillar of support.

Saylee Soundalgekar

A landscape architect and assistant professor by profession, Saylee believes in the power of storytelling. It is through this that architects can empower society and bring about a change in thinking and in policymaking. She locates her work at the juncture of natural landscapes, people, places and architecture, where there is great potential for sustainable living through narrative building. (ar.saylees@gmail.com)

Spalzen Angmo

Spalzen Angmo is currently pursuing her bachelor's in sociology and anthropology from St Xavier's College (Autonomous), Mumbai. (zinaamo22@gmail.com)

Shobhan Sachan

Shobhan is a creative explorer, passionate about observing and documenting intriguing subjects through sketching, photography and writing. With a background in architecture and urban planning, he delves into understanding the societal and cultural intricacies of settlement systems. He firmly believes that leveraging knowledge from the past and a deep study of the present is essential in synthesising impactful strategies for the future. (sachanshobhan@gmail.com)

Sonam Dechen

Sonam hails from Matho village. Presently, she works at the Himalayan Cultural Heritage Foundation. She harbours a deep passion for photography. To her, capturing moments through photos is a timeless way to preserve memories. Ladakh, with its rich cultural heritage and intriguing stories handed down from previous generations, has always captivated her.
(sonamdechen63@gmail.com)

Vaishnavi Subramanya

Vaishnavi is a twenty-four-year-old recently graduated kid with one foot in the real world and the other in fantasy. Being in architecture school made her fall back in love with history and theory. She loves telling stories, whether they are through words or visuals. Having grown up in the 2000s in Bengaluru, her inspirations come from everyday activities and the usual banter. An architect by profession and a traveller by passion, she currently works with a travelling architecture firm. (vaishnavi.iyer6@gmail.com)

About People Place Project

The People Place Project is an initiative dedicated to raising awareness about our environment, communities, and places through the lens of 'people' and 'empathy'. Through publications and pedagogy, we aim to create meaningful interventions that deepen our understanding of places and communities.

Founded in 2014 as People Called Mumbai, the project set out to explore the collective narrative of a place through the stories of its people. By 2020, the initiative had expanded significantly, resulting in the publication of over twenty books. The narrative mapping project, the 'People Called...' series, has since explored cities such as Ahmedabad, Shillong, Kolkata, Lucknow, Delhi, and Kochi. This framework has also been employed to archive the Kalaghoda Arts Festival and conduct numerous mapping exercises and workshops, such as Its Playtime, Stories by Sea, Divisive Landscapes, and as a method to intimately map human geographies.

Since 2020, we have broadened our scope with illustrated books, such as the City Mosaic series, Paani Party, Batata, Pao, and All Things Portuguese, and Happiness City. We have also actively collaborated with NGOs and Government organizations for curating and editing publications related to the built environment, such as the Heritage Handbooks and maps designed as tools to explore the heritage of metropolitan Mumbai in collaboration with MMRDA.

Ethnographic research has been foundational to our work. Our latest endeavor, Awaaz - Voices from Govandi, is a unique attempt at co-writing narratives with the residents, thus documenting a resettlement colony in Mumbai. For further details about our projects, please visit our website at www.peopleplaceproject.com.

About the Curators

Nisha Nair

Nisha Nair-Gupta is an architect, urban researcher and writer, and is currently a PhD research scholar in the Centre of Urban Science and Engineering at IIT–Bombay, Mumbai. She spearheads the publishing initiative, People Place Project, which has been invested in urban research, pedagogy and publication since its inception. As part of a publication initiative looking at creating literature, books, writing and media on urban consciousness, her responsibilities are editorial, creative and growth strategies. She has published five books as a curator and editor. Her current research works look at social spaces and urban mobilities, within the context of Southern urbanism. (nairnisha2306@gmail.com)

Shashi Velath

Shashi Velath is the CEO of Tinge of Green, an ecosystem enabler and builder within the sustainability solutions space. A renowned war and investigative journalist, he has earned prestigious awards such as the Ramnath Goenka Award and a Green Oscar. Transitioning into the social sector, he led international non-profits in fostering cross-sector collaborations and addressing complex societal challenges. With a passion for designing innovative strategies for sustainable development goals, Shashi now spearheads Tinge of Green's mission. The organisation focuses on fostering collaboration, innovation and growth within the sustainability sector through platforms, investments, partnerships, research support, policy advocacy, education and sustainability. (shashikumar.vk8@gmail.com)

www.ingramcontent.com/pod-product-compliance
Lightning Source LLC
LaVergne TN
LVHW021316200726

843509LV00002B/56